D0050692

Garvey

STEVE GARVEY

Garvey

WITH SKIP ROZIN

Times
BOOKS

Library of Congress Cataloging in Publication Data
Garvey, Steve, 1948–
Garvey.
1. Garvey, Steve, 1948–
2. Baseball players—United States—Biography.
I. Rozin, Skip.   II. Title.
GV865.G34A34   1986   796.357'092'4 [B]   85-40734
ISBN 0-8129-1272-1
Manufactured in the United States of America
First Edition

For Krisha and Whitney,
with all my love and dedication
DAD

Acknowledgments

Although the pages that follow contain Steve Garvey's story, many people have assisted me in helping him tell that story. I am indebted to all of them.

First, my thanks go to those who have influenced Steve's life and made this book more complete by talking of that, to Danny Litwhiler and Monsignor Lawrence Higgins, to Guy Welman, Ken Nuznoff and Monty Basgal.

I want to thank Millie and Joe Garvey, Jerry Kapstein, Alan Rothenberg, Jeri Burbank and especially John Boggs, the glue of that California contingent and the project's ace troubleshooter.

My special thanks go to Steve's teammates, past and present, and to the teams who have given me a chance to hear their stories, to the Yankees and the Mets, the Dodgers and the Phillies, and mostly to the San Diego Padres. Without the active support of

ACKNOWLEDGMENTS

Ballard Smith and Jack McKoen, of John "Doc" Mattei, of Mike Swanson and Bill Beck, there would be no book.

When writing about sports, most of the background material comes from the daily journalists who cover that beat. The work of Tom Friend, Barry Bloom, Phil Collier and others covering the Padres and Dodgers made my job easier.

Which brings me to Jonathan Segal, who brought Steve and me together for this project and has helped smooth the road ever since, to Basil Kane, and to James Brown, who guided me through the early stages.

Personally, I wish to express my continued appreciation to Joan Ross Acocella. And, of course, to Julie Guibord.

Skip Rozin

Garvey

1

It was one of those 5 o'clock starts in San Diego, when the pitcher's mound is in bright sunshine and home plate is in shadow. Pascual Perez was pitching for Atlanta in the first game of a double header. He's a sidearm "slinger"—the toughest kind of guy to hit against in conditions like that. The first pitch, a fastball, exploded from third base. I never saw it.

The truth is, I was tired. Not just road-tired, though there was some of that. We'd just had a day off after a night game in Pittsburgh, and I'd flown into New York to see my daughters. Since Cyndy and I separated and she'd been working in New York, I tried to fly in whenever I could, like an off day anywhere east of St. Louis. I stayed at the Parker Meridien. The girls and I swam in the hotel pool, did some shopping, had a fun day. After a long road trip it was energizing to see them, so I stayed over that night and flew out the next morning. It was 1 o'clock before I reached San Diego, hardly time for lunch before getting to the park. Everything was rushed.

But I was more than just tired from travel. There had been nine months of turmoil. Ending my career with Los Angeles after fifteen seasons, with all the tension and emotion involved; flying around the country talking with different clubs who were interested in signing me, and the difficult negotiations at the end (in all those seasons in baseball, I had never dealt with anybody but the Dodgers). Finally—signing with San Diego just before Christmas, then trying to settle in before spring training, finding a place to live, dealing with a thousand details. Then boom, there's the season, and there's The Streak. Eleven games in, I broke Billy Williams' National League record for consecutive games. In Los Angeles. Before a packed house. With a standing ovation that lasted two full minutes, the crowd chanting "GAR-VEY! GAR-VEY!" It was very emotional. I knew full well that in the history of baseball, only two men had been more durable, Gehrig and Everett Scott, and I would surely catch Scott within a year. The whole season was charged with electricity. By the 100th game—that's when it happened, in the 100th game—I was tired through to my soul.

Perez threw the second pitch in the dirt, then threw one I missed completely. I was really having trouble with the sun. He threw another sidearm sinker. I fouled it off and was 2 and 2. Now I had to make contact. The next pitch I barely saw. I swung and topped it down the third base line and beat it out, no play. With two strikes, the third baseman, Bob Horner, had been back.

Suddenly I was at third. One run was in, and we had two men out. The second pitch to Garry Templeton was a fastball, way up. Bruce Benedict, the catcher, never touched it, and I headed for home. Normally in that situation I'd score standing up, but behind home plate in San Diego there is a padded area in case the catcher comes back for a pop-up—protection so he doesn't get hurt. The ball hit the padding just right and bounced halfway back to home plate, which meant that the catcher only had to turn around and go about fifteen feet.

I was coming down the line and Perez was straddling home plate, waiting for the ball. He's a tall, skinny kid, six-two or six-three, maybe 165 pounds. I knew if I came straight in I was going to catch his leg or buckle his knee, so I tried to slide around and get my toe in, but he tagged me before I got to the plate.

I put my hand back for support and felt my thumb—something happened—and then my hand went into the dirt and he tagged me.

The umpire called me out, and as everybody rushed off the field, I was still on my knees, holding my left thumb. I felt it was dislocated, so I put it back in place and thought to myself, We can tape it up and I'll be able to play. We'll ice it down and maybe I can just play a little of the second game. I'll be fine tomorrow.

It was a typical between innings—people running off the field, people coming on. I stood up and looked at my thumb. I took my right hand away and the thumb just fell down. The pain was starting. I tried to lift the thumb and couldn't. I moved it up into a normal position with my right hand and then let go. Again it fell.

By then Dick Dent, the Padres' trainer, was standing with me between home and first. Our manager, Dick Williams, joined him. They helped me walk toward the dugout. The tag had been in the shadows, but by the time I walked down the first base line I was in the sun, and it was hot. I remember there being a hush. Usually between innings everybody is getting up and moving around, going to the toilet, getting something to eat. Somebody told me later that many of the fans were standing—most were watching me.

When I reached the tunnel that leads from the dugout to the clubhouse, everything hit me. I could feel the blood drain from my face. I broke into a sweat and had to drop down to my knees. My stomach started to feel queasy.

I remember feeling very lonely, very, very lonely. There were people close around and they were concerned about me—Williams, my teammates, our trainer—but it was like no one else was there.

There was pain in my thumb and in the wrist area, but I had always prided myself on being able to tolerate pain. I had played with pain. This was something else. It was more of a pain in my heart. The Streak had been the biggest commitment of my life, and all of a sudden that commitment and everything I'd had for all those 1,207 games were gone.

The Streak: it takes on a life of its own. You have to have lived it to understand. Billy Williams knows, but nobody else. Seven years, never missing a game. You think about the cuts and the sprains, the times, hobbled by a pulled hamstring, you struggled to the plate to bat, to help your team—and to extend The Streak. You think about the luck, the times you could have been injured seriously and weren't. And the other times, like just before the strike in 1981, when I had a sprained wrist and couldn't drive the ball. It got so bad that finally, in the ninth inning, I suggested that Tom Lasorda put in Reggie Smith for me. I would have had to sit out, but the next day the strike started, and I got six weeks to recuperate.

The Streak: it becomes everything. But it takes a toll. It's preparing yourself physically, mentally, playing with pain, the good days and the bad days. Professional decisions, social decisions, even personal decisions—everything comes second.

There were times I could have stayed out of games, maybe even should have. I probably should have stayed with my daughter Whitney at the emergency room after she fell out of a tree and broke her arm. But I stayed until I knew she was going to be okay, then left and made it to the game just in time to go out onto the field.

All that places an enormous amount of pressure on a family. I know Cyndy felt it; it's a hard way to live. Williams ended his streak himself because he thought it was too much of a burden. He just took himself out one day in September. With Gehrig, he had to be dying to sit out. For me it was a thumb.

How ironic. You might think it would be a big collision somewhere, or something equally dramatic. But to have a thumb be the reason! Maybe it was God's way of adding a little perspective.

They rushed me to Ida May Green Hospital for X rays. Waiting for the results, I still thought maybe it was just stretched—maybe they could tape it, and then I could get back for the second game. Maybe it was okay.

Within a few minutes Paul Hirschman, one of the Padres' three doctors, came out and said it was a torn ligament. He said it would be best to operate. Sometimes no operation is performed; patients can end up with something called gatekeeper's thumb, or skier's thumb. But if your thumb is vital to your profession, you operate. They put on a plaster cast and scheduled surgery for the following morning.

I rode back to the stadium with John Boggs, my friend and business associate, and we listened to the radio. The announcers for the game were saying, "Well, we don't know what the prognosis is. He might be back for the second game. We just don't know."

That's how it was—all the attention focused on the streak. So much talk, so much conjecture, everybody asking, "Are you going to break Gehrig's record?" or, "How far are you going to go?" I would have needed to play through a third of the 1989 season to match Gehrig's 2,130, and I don't think I ever considered that realistic.

Back at the stadium, they were all waiting—AP, UPI, the television stations, radio, the newspapers—with tape machines rolling and cameras flashing. It was tough. I tried to smile for them and be philosophical. I thought I was. But later, when I saw the pictures, while I was giving the "thumbs up," I wasn't smiling.

They operated the following morning, a team headed by Dr. Merlin Hamer of the Scripps Clinic in San Diego. It all went very well. It was clean, a clean tear. They kept me in the hospital overnight, and the next day I began an unwelcome summer vacation.

It was a very strange time. Not only was the streak over—I didn't even have baseball. Very difficult for someone whose life is built around 162 games a year. It was hard not to be around the game itself, not to be able to get out on the field and be part of it. But the cast was going to be on for seven weeks. I had to find some way of keeping involved.

For the front office, it was easy. There are always public relations opportunities. I did some color commentary for local television. They were doing some testing for cable telecasts, and I worked some of them, too. Then I started to learn more about the organization and began making suggestions, whether about promotion or travel accommodations or what needed to be done during spring training—things I'd learned from Los Angeles.

It was a little harder with the team itself. I couldn't catch, so I couldn't pitch batting practice. I couldn't get out in the boxes and coach; we have coaches. I couldn't be a batting instructor; at that time of the year there was someone to do that. It was a delicate situation.

I decided on a plan. There wasn't much I could do on the road, but I made it my responsibility to attend every home game, to be there but maintain a low profile. I showed up about an hour and a half before game time, making myself available if anybody wanted to talk to me, but not forcing it.

With these guys, that was easy. We ended up talking a lot about baseball, about skills, about execution. This had rarely happened on the Dodgers, and it always bothered me. After all the years of success and batting over .300, hitting for power and hitting and running and bunting and whatever, few in Los Angeles ever asked me anything about what I thought. I don't know why. Either they felt I couldn't relate to them or they felt they couldn't approach me.

During those weeks there was also a lot of business to take care of. I had moved my office down to San Diego from Los Angeles; I went in there every morning. Soon I began working out. Even with the cast on, I ran, and once it was off I started a program of stretching the hand, stretching the ligament, getting myself ready for spring training.

All that was good and necessary, and when I look back on those weeks, I count them as productive. At the same time, something else was happening, something more important. Taking off those 62 games acted as a punctuating point in my career, in my life. I needed that—I didn't realize how much. It wasn't only that year that was so hectic; the pace had been getting faster and faster for a long time. From 1977 or 1978 on, life had started to get more complex on many fronts. It was almost as if things had gotten out of control.

I remember the plane ride after we'd won the World Series in 1981, after the sixth game, heading back from New York to Los Angeles. It was for me the best and worst of times. The best because we had finally won a championship, after losing in '74 to

Oakland and losing twice to New York in '77 and '78. The best because of how we won: being down two games to Houston in the mini-playoff and coming back; being down two to one to Montreal in the league championships and winning that; dropping the first two to New York in the Series, then rallying to win four straight. You couldn't invent a better script. But it was the worst of times because my wife and I were separated, and she and my two daughters were in Manhattan. I had won there where they were living; I knew they were only a few miles away, and we weren't together.

Pressure on the marriage had been building for three or four years. There was a growing frustration that both of our lives were becoming very active, very busy, with extraneous demands. The girls were starting to get a little older, and they were very demanding. Cyndy had her career; I had my career. We both had a marriage and children, and no time. It's not that she didn't love me or I didn't love her, but there were no answers to our problems, and there needed to be answers. But what? Could I quit baseball, or commit less of myself to it than I always had? Could she quit her job in television? Life together started to become draining, physically and mentally.

It was about then that *Inside Sports* happened along. I was told they wanted to do a feature on me that would include material on how Cyndy and I coordinated our busy lives. It ended up as a scathing personal attack on us and our life-style—even on our furniture and the pictures in our house. That's why we took them to court.

What the article did to us, mostly, was to take a difficult situation and make it even more tense. Eventually, in September of 1981, Cyndy took the girls and moved to New York. Cyndy thinks the marriage broke up because I was involved with another woman, someone who worked for me, but I wasn't seeing anyone else back then, before she left. I think all those pressures—the public attention from my career and her career—drove us apart.

So by that October, with all the elation of a World Series victory, I was going back to an empty house.

On that plane ride, everybody was so excited, and then everybody just kind of collapsed, pooh! It was about 3 o'clock, and they were all asleep. We still had a couple of hours left before Los Angeles. It was very quiet.

I stood in the back of the plane and thought about how I had finally accomplished what I had set out to accomplish, realizing the dream I had had as a boy. I had been the Dodger bat boy in spring training so, many seasons before, and now I was the first baseman of the world championship team after being frustrated for three World Series. And I was playing the position of Gil Hodges, who had been my boyhood idol. I still have a photograph of the two of us together.

How lucky I was. I thought back to when I was a kid in Tampa, picking up little grapefruits and hitting them with a stick, hour after hour. I thought of all the hard work along the way from there to here, making the shift from third base to first, working on my fielding, working on my hitting, making myself a better ballplayer.

Here it was, the culmination of all that work, reaching the high point—and the low point, because I wasn't sharing it with the people I loved the most. There was a certain emptiness, a certain hollowness, to it. While I was focused so intently on one goal, something very dear that I thought was safely mine had slipped away.

When I think about that plane ride, I have to smile. There I was, marveling at all those changes, and the changes were only beginning. Never did I anticipate what was coming in the spring. After a championship season, I was looking forward to signing a new contract in 1982 with the Dodgers, one that would carry me through to the end of my career.

But after the holidays, there was no contact from the front office. Into spring training, no word. When finally during the spring there was conversation, it was "We'll talk," that kind of thing.

I knew the pressure would start to build, and it did. Every day. With every team that came over to Vero Beach, there was a new city's press. Chicago. Philadelphia. New York. What was happening? they all asked. What was I going to do?

Then, in the last ten days of spring training, I pulled a hamstring and stayed back when the team went to St. Petersburg. I was in the training room one afternoon when the phone rang. It was Peter O'Malley, the Dodger president. He asked me to meet him over at the airport, on the runway where the team plane usually stands.

Thirty minutes later I drove up next to his car on the runway. I got out of my car and into his. He said they very much wanted to sign me but had a policy about not signing a player before his contract was up. I said I'd rather begin negotiations and come to some agreement, that I was getting a lot of pressure. His only answer was that we should have a policy of no comment, and I said that would be impossible. I'd always had direct communication with the press.

That was that, for the rest of the spring and most of the season. There were negotiations, but I never felt the organization was totally committed to signing me. I knew what was happening: Many of us had come up together, and we were veterans now. The Dodgers, looking to the future, were ready to clean house. I had seen it happen to others, and now it was happening to me.

Psychologically, that period was the greatest burden of my life. It showed. I didn't have a very good season on the field, and my batting average was the lowest in ten years.

And when the new season began, I was gone.

Being a Dodger meant so very much to me—it was part of how I defined myself. You would think that changing that would be the kind of punctuation point I needed, but it wasn't. Even after I left, the streak kept some of that feeling alive. It was The Dodger Streak, begun as a Dodger. When I broke the record, I did it back at Dodger Stadium, getting all that affection from my fans in Los Angeles.

But when the streak ended, it all ended. A major chapter of my life ended. In a way, the injury was a great relief. I'm not sure, because of the way it happened, that there wasn't a certain destiny in it, a certain divine destiny telling me that it was time to take a break, to regroup.

Finally, the burden of the previous five seasons was over. Everything got resolved, one way or another. My marriage was over. My consecutive game streak was over. My career with the Dodgers was over. The three central focuses of my life over the most important period of my life were all over.

My reaction was not depression, but more acceptance. And there was exhilaration in the challenge: new team, new city, new streak. Everything fresh, like being a kid again. A little older, but still with time enough for renewal.

It may sound funny, but what I thought about a lot during those days was the first beginning. I thought about Tampa, and of old fantasies.

2

When I was playing baseball in high school, getting a lot of attention from television and newspaper reporters in central Florida—interviews and game highlights on the news; pictures and even headlines in the papers—people used to say to me, "Gee, you must think about being a big-league star all the time." Well, I really didn't. Not then. I knew I had some talent, but I had no idea how far it would take me.

Earlier, when I was just a little kid, seven, maybe eight years old, my head was filled with nothing else. Then is when I did my fantasizing. I was an only child, and there weren't a lot of kids my age in the area of Tampa where we lived. As a result, I spent an unusual amount of time alone. I didn't really mind; I had my games.

At night, just before going to bed, I would set up my lineups for the next day's play. I'd have my baseball cards right there in front of me, and I would write out the batting order for each team. If I put in a wrong number, or even if the names didn't look right—a little messy—I'd redo them, three or four times if necessary. I was meticulous.

The next day I would say that it was the first game of the World Series—or the third game or whatever—and I'd go out to the yard and play through the game, the whole game, every out, all by myself. I'd toss the ball up and swing. Three misses were an out; so was a pop-up. A shot into the tree was a single, off the wall a double, and if I reached the neighbor's yard, it was a homer. I'd try to play it even and square. Usually it was between the Yankees and the Dodgers, because they were my favorite teams. Invariably it would go to the seventh game, and the Dodgers always had a good chance of winning.

I was a good mimic, and I would swing like every player in the lineup. Roy Campanella had a stocky build, so he had a wider stance and more or less rotated with a short stride. Pee Wee Reese had his bat a little flatter because he was more of a contact hitter, hitting and running. Gil McDougald, on the Yankees, had a very distinct stance, where his elbows were sticking in different directions and his bat stuck up in the air. I could bat left-handed and right, but I concentrated on the right-handers, on Carl Furillo and Charlie Neal and Reese.

Invariably, during each of those games, I would find myself in the game-winning situation. I would always be getting up in the late innings with the big hit needed to win the game. And I always came through. Even if I threw the ball up three times and missed it, I'd stretch the truth enough to say I'd foul-tipped it, so I could get one more chance to come through.

I never wore a uniform for my games; there were no crowds. It was just me, as all those players in my lineup, winning the game.

It sounds strange, thinking about it now: a seven-year-old boy being that organized, laying out his baseball cards in the proper order, writing out the lineups so carefully. But that's how it was. That's how my world was then—very organized. My mother worked; my father worked; and I had chores to do. From early morning till the last thing at night, everything was set up so that things ran smoothly.

When I was six, my mother worked as a secretary for an insurance company, and my father drove a bus for the city of Tampa. He had to be at work at 6 o'clock, and my mother drove him. Every morning at 5:30 I would climb into the backseat of the family Ford with my pillow and my blanket and sleep while my mother drove my dad to work, then come home and go back to sleep in my bed till it was time for school.

After school there were chores. I would report to my grandmother's house and do whatever I could to help her.

Both my parents are from Long Island. When my mother was a little girl, her mother was in a freak accident. She was walking down the road when a tire came flying off a truck and hit her in the back. It left her with neurological problems: She could walk, but she couldn't use her arms and hands properly; they were stiff and rigid. And she was subject to colds and lung infections. These got worse as she got older, and finally the doctors said it would be better if she left the north. So she and my grandfather moved to Tampa, and my mother and dad decided to go too, to be near them. That was about a month before I was born.

Anyhow, when I was old enough—maybe seven—and my mom was working, it was my job to go over after school and help my grandmother. She tried to do things herself, but it was very difficult. She vacuumed by putting the handle of the cleaner between her stiff arms and pushing it around. It took forever to do the house. She would iron, which still amazes me. She used to take the iron, and push it with her straight arms and hands that were almost useless. When she finished a section of shirt she'd move it with her teeth. This was not only time-consuming and tedious, but dangerous. She had no feeling in her fingers, and occasionally she would slip and touch the hot iron, burning herself without knowing.

She couldn't go to the bathroom by herself; I'd have to help her. Sometimes she couldn't get up, or she couldn't wipe herself. It wasn't anything I thought about much. I just did it because she was my grandma and she needed help; she was "Nanny."

I would come in after school, vacuum, straighten up, do whatever she needed. Then I'd start dinner, following her instructions. Peel the potatoes, open cans. If it was a meat meal, it would usually be stew, and I could prepare that with all the seasonings. Chicken was my specialty; bake at 415 degrees for an hour and fifteen minutes.

After I was finished I'd go off to baseball practice, but I'd come back and play around her house till my grandfather came home from work. If my grandmother needed me, she'd signal by ringing a bell tied to the end of a string or by flashing the porch light off and on.

I really liked her. Her handicap never eased, never let up on her, but she wasn't bitter or angry. She was a sweet person.

At home I had other responsibilities. I had to keep my room clean and help keep the house straight. I'd empty the garbage, help with the dishes, wash the car on Saturday, and, when I got older, cut the grass. My dad liked a neat lawn. He would cut it during the week if he was home, but the St. Augustine grass grows fast during the summer, so I'd have to cut it a second time.

The point is, we were a *family*, and we all had something to do to make things work. There was no outside help. We divided up the chores among ourselves, and everyone did his or her share. Organization made it all work smoothly.

During those years, sports were my only recreation. The faster I could get done with my homework and chores, the faster I could go out and play. And what I loved most was baseball. Whether playing on the local Little League team or by myself in the back yard—it was always baseball for me.

My father started me, playing catch with me when I was about six. He had played baseball on Long Island—first base, actually—and was serious enough about football to play defensive tackle along with one of my uncles on a semipro team. When I was seven, the first Little League started in our area, and my dad went to the initial meetings. I played that year; normally you have to be eight, but they needed players.

Ours was the Drew Park Little League—that was where we lived. Drew Park was an old naval base that had been converted into a residential section. The field and school were about a mile and a half away. I had a blue Schwinn that took me everywhere.

That first year I played for the Cardinals, and my position was right field. I remember not catching too many balls out there, but running them down until they stopped rolling, then throwing them in. The first pop-up I ever thought I had a chance for was short, and I came running in, thinking I had it all the way. I ended up knocking down the second baseman as the ball fell to the ground. Everybody laughed.

My offense wasn't too strong, either. That whole first year I never got a hit. Batted zero. In maybe twelve, fourteen games I got only five or six official at-bats because I walked so much. I wasn't very tall, and I'd crouch way down. With a strike zone of maybe six inches, no pitcher that age had the control to get the ball over. And I was quick, so I scored a lot of runs. My first hit came two years into the game. It was a semi-line drive between third and short that hit the back of the dirt and rolled into the outfield. A 2 and 2 pitch, I think.

There were other sports, too: football and basketball. When I was nine, I started playing golf. But nothing compared with baseball. Baseball was my first love, because of the Dodgers—the Brooklyn Dodgers. They were very big in my life.

It started with my grandfather—my father's father—who grew up in Brooklyn and was a diehard Dodger fan. He moved to Long Island and became a policeman in Rockville Center. He used to talk about walking his beat during the summer, how every merchant had the ballgame on radio. You'd hear Red Barber's voice in the barber shop, Red Barber's voice in the delicatessen. With everybody's window open, it was early stereo.

One spring day when I was seven and my father had started driving for Greyhound, he came home one night and told me that the next day he was going to drive for the Dodgers. Then he asked if I would like to bat-boy. Well, I said, sure, I'd love to. But I have school. He said he thought I could miss school, because being a bat boy had so much more social value than anything I would learn in school that day. I wasn't sure what he meant, but I agreed.

The night before, I couldn't think of anything else. I laid out my light blue jeans, my tennis shoes, my Ban-lon shirt. I didn't know whether to wear a hat or not. I had a flat-top then, and I used so much butch wax that my hair was sticking straight up.

I got up earlier than my dad and was waiting when he was ready at 7 o'clock. On the way to pick up the bus, and then going to the airport, I was full of questions. Should I shake the guy's hand at home plate after he hits a home run or wait till he shakes mine? Should I play catch with the guys?

My father told me just to relax. "Let's not put too much theatrics into this," he said.

It was like doing anything else you haven't done before. You don't know where to move or where to stand. You don't want to get in anybody's way. And this was so special. These were the Brooklyn Dodgers, and I was seven years old.

The first man off the plane was Lee Scott, the traveling secretary, followed by Walter Alston, the manager. Of course I didn't recognize either one, but I would get to know them later. Then the players started off. I remember seeing Pee Wee Reese and Roy Campanella—he was winning Most Valuable Player awards in those years. Then Jackie Robinson and Carl Furillo, Gil Hodges, Charlie Neal, and then the pitchers.

I recognized maybe half of them that first morning, and the recognition factor increased once we got to the park and they had their uniforms on. I remember standing inside the dressing room, right by the door, watching with big eyes, listening with big ears.

Later, it was my job to carry the batbag out to the dugout. It must have weighed one hundred pounds, and I couldn't budge it, but one of the guys helped me. Once outside, I straightened all the bats up—in fact, I was meticulous. I put them in a straight line on the ground and arranged all the helmets just right. Of course, within five minutes of batting practice everything was all over; bats, helmets, everywhere. But I didn't care. When batting practice was over, I lined up all the equipment again. It was a great day.

Two or three other times that first year I went with my dad and got to work as a bat boy; another time for the Dodgers and once for the Yankees. I'd get an occasional pat on the head as the players boarded the bus, but they more or less ignored me. I stood down in the little stairwell, out of everybody's way, and listened hard to what was being said, trying to remember every word, every story. Later, at home, I'd have a hundred questions for my dad about what they'd said. Sometimes, when it was a baseball term, like "keystone combination" or "squeeze bunt," he gave me the definition. Otherwise, when it was some other colorful term, he'd just say, "Well, let's wait a while on that." There were a lot of "wait a whiles."

The players really liked my dad. Not just because he's warm and congenial, though that was part of it. He was such a good bus driver. He did all the little things. He got the bus right up to the stairs of the plane—nobody had done that before. He was always there on time, and the bus was already ready and cooled off after the game.

They got to know him and requested him on every trip over from Vero Beach after that first year. They tipped him well. Whenever I could, I would go along with him—mostly on weekends, two, maybe three times during the spring. Sometimes he'd drive for the Yankees; I was a bat boy for them a few times, too, and once for Detroit.

After two or three years, the Dodgers started remembering my name, which was the biggest compliment a bat boy could have. And sometimes they'd include me in practice, just a little. Once during a workout I was catching the ball for Pete Reiser. He was back with the team as a coach, and was hitting shots to the out-fielders. Frank Howard, who had just come up, was playing in the field, throwing line drives right in. They'd short-hop me, but I'd make the catch. Reiser yelled at him, "Would you take it easy on the kid? You're going to kill him."

I was proud of myself for making the catches and thrilled to be included in their clowning.

By the time I was eleven or twelve, I had started to develop a kind of all-American attitude about how athletes were supposed to act. There were a lot of good qualities I could see in a Reese, a Hodges: a certain amount of confidence, of leadership. Not flashy, but solid.

Like Jim Gilliam, sitting at the corner of the dugout, on the steps, chewing his bubble gum, really cracking it loud and blowing bubbles as if he didn't have a care in the world. Every spring there would be some young phenom there to take his job; every spring a new hotshot. Gilliam would sit there chewing his gum, go in the last two innings, then the next day come back and work hard before the game. He never said much, and within a week or two he'd be back at his old job.

When teammates approached one of these men, they did so with respect. When they spoke of them, they spoke with respect. I began to define "leader" less as a showy star and more as a solid player other men came to for advice, for guidance. Maybe the players didn't use those words, but that was what they meant. In a game-ending situation, these leaders were the players their teammates looked to. With a one-run lead in the ninth inning, they wanted the ball hit to Pee Wee. When they were behind with time running out, you'd hear, "Two more hitters till Gil." That was a pretty good testimony.

There were other things that I began to see, things not happening on the field. Before and after games, when coming off the bus or going on, I used to listen to how the players treated the fans. I was only ten or eleven, but how they behaved mattered to me.

While reactions were purely individual, some players—like Reese and Hodges—were always better with the fans than others. They seemed to always have the time. Some of the other guys, some who didn't play that much, had neither time nor tolerance. They'd sign one or two autographs, and that would be it. Some couldn't be bothered signing any; they'd go right to the bus as if nobody were there. (I've actually seen guys hide from fans, just to avoid signing a slip of paper.) Some were second-line players; others were big stars. It made an impression.

Of course, the quintessential baseball player for me was Hodges. First of all, he was so much like my father. They were similar in size, both about six-two. They both had big hands and were soft-spoken. Both hard-working. People looked up to them. My father's friends really admire him; fans felt the same way about Hodges. It was his demeanor, his personality, the way he walked and carried himself. It was the air he had about him.

Like I tell kids now, hopefully their father is the number-one man in their life, their hero. But there have to be reinforcements, other people, with strong, positive beliefs, whom children can look up to. Gil was that person for me. He reinforced what my father stood for. While I didn't know it then, there was this trinity forming. My dad played first base; Hodges played first. Eventually, I would, too.

Since Hodges was right there at first base, he was always relatively close to the dugout, close to my station. We had more contact, and I could feel the warmth of the man. He used to ask me how school was going and how I was getting along in Little League. He took an interest. When he came out to the field after dressing, he'd always play catch with me. I try to do that with kids now, and I always have since I came up with the Dodgers. I think they appreciate it; it'll be a memory for them, the way playing catch with Hodges is for me.

That behavior—the kindness, the responsiveness to the fans—said all the more to me when contrasted with the actions of those players who didn't sign autographs, who had no time for the people. Maybe it wasn't because they didn't want to. Maybe there was a lot of pressure on them in their jobs, and they felt they had to concentrate on being the best they could.

I didn't understand those things then. I was young and a purist. I thought everybody should say hello to somebody who says hello first. You exchange greetings—that is basic common respect for one another. My father was that way; my mother was that way. All their friends were that way. Nobody ever put it into words as a rule, but they acted it.

The time spent with the Dodgers—I'm talking about three or four times each spring over six or seven years—made baseball seem very wonderful to me. The game itself, the excitement of being around real stars, was transferred to my own game. Even in the beginning, when I was no star myself, it was wonderful.

It rains a lot in Florida—Tampa Bay has more thunderstorms than any other place in America—and I can see myself at eight, standing out in right field, puddles of water up to my ankles, loving every minute.

Learning to hit took me a while, but I continued to work at it all during that first year and into the second. Even inside, when it was cold and rainy. I'd make a little ball out of bits of paper and wrap tape around it, then hit it with a good, strong pencil. Talk about pitching yourself tight—I couldn't pitch myself away because I'd never reach the ball. When I did connect, the ball couldn't hurt anything.

For playing outside with other kids, I'd make a bigger ball using more paper and more tape, and hit it with a broomstick. It would last for a couple of days; then the paper would start to come out through the tape, and I'd have to tape it again, and again. When it got wet and then dried, it would get hard, but at only about a sixth the size of a baseball. It wouldn't travel that far, and so it wasn't destructive.

Then there were the cork balls, made from a wine cork wrapped with tape. They were the toughest to hit, because they were so light. They would sink or sail as they came in, and it was difficult to hit them squarely. When you did connect just right, it'd be like a propellor, generating a lot of spin and not going very far.

Later, we moved from Drew Park to a wonderful neighborhood a couple of miles north, a place with quiet streets and houses set back on wide lawns. There was no house next door, just a big yard with thirteen fruit trees. Little grapefruits were everywhere, some the size of big marbles, some a little larger, and hard. I'd collect maybe fifty or sixty in a bucket and use them for batting practice, throwing them up and hitting them, hour after hour.

That was probably the best exercise for eye-hand coordination, because I used a stick instead of a bat, and I did so much of it. I see the effects today. You can't take a real big swing with those little grapefruits. Just toss one up and hit it. I developed a good, quick stroke.

Baseball had its effect academically, too. In first grade I was a very poor reader. By the time I was in third grade I was the top reader in my class, simply because sports stimulated my interest. I read everything on athletics I could find: sports sections in the newspaper and the John Tunis books—*World Series* and *All-American*. I read Bernard Malamud's book *The Natural,* though I had a little trouble with that.

Those early years were so important. Even at seven and eight, I was learning about attitude. I knew hitting was a craft and had to be worked on. I learned that from the Dodgers, watching them practice before games, listening to them taking instruction from teammates and coaches. I was working, too. Even when there were no other kids around, I used my little games to get better.

My second year in Little League, while I still hadn't gotten a hit, I was swinging more. With more swings came more contact, and with contact, eventually, came my first hit. That first one, of course, was a breakthrough, and I began improving rapidly. I moved to second base the next year and started to hit with consistency. It wasn't long before I made my first all-star team.

Even at that age, nine years old, I knew something had happened. I could feel my own aggressiveness and a certain leadership quality. In football, I was the quarterback, making plays and scoring. In basketball, I was the play-making guard. In baseball, I moved to shortstop and also did some pitching.

Every one of those positions is where the young athlete plays who is separating himself from the pack. Those are the positions of leadership at nine and ten years of age. That's how you gain confidence: by putting yourself in pressure situations, asking yourself to come through when the game is on the line.

There was one game when I was about ten. I was playing for a league championship all-star team. It was a preliminary round for the city championships, maybe the quarterfinals. I was pitching. I gave up a home run to the first man up in the first inning, then for six innings registered fifteen out of eighteen outs by strikeouts. In the meantime we scored a run, which I knocked in, so the game was tied.

The manager asked me how I felt, and I said I didn't know. I'd never pitched more than six innings before, but I thought I was okay. I went back to the mound in the seventh and struck out two more.

I pitched the eighth and ninth as well, bringing my strikeout record to twenty-two of twenty-seven batters for the game, and I almost hit a home run in the ninth to win the game. The guy caught it at the fence; I think the wind was blowing in.

In the tenth inning we brought in another pitcher, and they scored three runs to beat us, four to one. But that was a turning point. I knew I had something I could rely on, a reserve of talent and energy never before tested. I'd crossed a barrier. All of a sudden those old fantasies of mine—batting balls in the back yard as Roy Campanella or Gil Hodges, knocking in the winning run in the final game of the World Series—were being turned into real-life possibilities. And I liked them.

I didn't know then how hard it was to become a professional athlete (Tampa wasn't exactly a hotbed of future stars in the 1950s). I had never been exposed to the stories of young men who'd signed pro contracts and had gone away filled with hope and promise, only to be broken by the experience of failure. Success was still possible to me, and I saw no reason why I couldn't have it.

I was never one to talk of such things, not openly among my friends, but being a big-leaguer was on my mind all the time, day and night. I don't even know if my parents knew; I kept these thoughts in a very private part of me.

From Mildred Garvey, Steve's mother:

"Steve was about nine or ten when we asked him what he would like for Christmas. He said a new baseball glove, so I told him to go down to the store and pick out the one he wanted. I expected a boy that age to choose a glove for five or six dollars, but when I asked him where he'd seen the glove and how much it cost, he told me twenty-five dollars. I was shocked. That was a lot of money, and I told him so.

"He said 'Mom, look at it this way: twenty-five dollars now will bring you twenty-five thousand later on.'

"What did I do? I went out and bought the glove. I couldn't turn that down."

3

As I moved into my teens, I was becoming a pretty good baseball player. But by then I was less sure about becoming a professional. Oh, it was always in the back of my mind, but I tried to keep it there. I knew I had talent, but athletic ability, especially at the high school level, is so difficult to evaluate. How far would mine take me?

Those early dreams of glory in the big leagues were now clouded by reality. I knew just how many guys were out there trying for the same thing, and how few jobs were available. I knew of high school ballplayers who had signed with fanfare, then been released after a season or two in the minors. Those are sad stories.

My focus was on college. I wanted to become a good enough

player to earn a scholarship. It could be for baseball; it could be for football. That didn't matter, as long as I got to college.

At the time I was placing a lot of value on my coaches. I looked up to them, admired them. They became my new role models, along with my father. I could see myself someday being a coach of young men, helping them, giving them guidance. I don't know if I thought about this then, but I was not only resisting thinking about becoming a ballplayer, I had also devised a plan of making up for some of the lost rewards. College and coaching—they were things I could count on.

If all this sounds unusually conservative, it was. Even I recognize that. Typically, any teenage athlete with a shot at being drafted would be full of his own chances. I was much more practical. That was how I was raised. Practicality was the main theme in our household.

Just as finishing the dishes was my pass to play, getting good grades in school was my pass to sports. I may have dearly loved baseball and football, but I had been made to understand that their primary value was in earning me a scholarship. My parents and I discussed college sports as a vehicle to a pro career, but that had to come later. The order of priorities was firm.

In all areas, I was a very practical, a very cautious young man. At ten and eleven, when kids were shoplifting for kicks, I wanted no part of it. At thirteen and fourteen, when they started smoking, I never did. The idea turned me off. That's probably why pot never interested me—because I didn't smoke. I didn't need drugs either. I got myself high on what I was doing, on sports and people. It may sound corny, but that was how I felt. I still do.

I never drank at all till college, and then only an occasional beer. To this day I'd rather have a glass of iced tea. I'm not saying I never drink. I may have a beer with dinner, or an occasional glass of wine. Rarely anything more.

There were times along the way when my attitudes set me apart. That last year of high school, the guys thought they were big-time when they'd go out Saturday nights and drink. Sometimes they'd get together and run to somebody's lake house for a beer party. They'd invite me, but I would pass. It was against the rules then—against the coaches' rules—so I didn't want to be part of it. Besides, I didn't enjoy things like that.

You might think it was a big problem, especially at that age, but it wasn't. I'm sure people considered me square, but most of these guys were my friends—two or three of them good friends. And I always played well enough, and performed well enough, for them to respect my ability.

My dating habits were conservative, too. I was monogamous at a time when a lot of my friends were not. I was never one to hop around, to date this girl on Friday and that girl on Saturday. I found somebody I liked, I stayed with her, and only when it ended for one reason or another did I move on.

Sex wasn't something that was a main interest to me, either. It was a dangerous situation. Besides, it was something I thought about in connection with marriage. Although there was this one girl during my junior year. She was a little wilder, a little more aggressive. But that ended. I always had the idea, somewhere in the back of my mind, that I really couldn't get serious about a girl because I had things to do. I was going to go off to college.

I think back and I have to smile. There was a thick core of seriousness running through me at a time when seriousness is supposed to be the furthest thing from a boy's mind. I even dressed the part. No torn blue jeans, T-shirt, and dirty white sneakers for me. They kidded me about my wing-tipped shoes when I came up to the Dodgers. But it started long before that. Back in high school it was loafers—Bass Weejuns, of course. Hagar slacks, Gant shirts—button-down collars and starched stiff. I like to be neat.

In an interview, my father had this to say on the subject:

"You'd have to say he was neat. The players on the bus, before they knew his name, referred to him as that neat little kid. Even at ten years old, he was concerned about how he looked. Sometimes even fussy.

"Once when he was just a little fellow, Millie was feeling under the weather, and so I did the ironing. I'd never ironed before, but I gave it a try. And I did okay.

"A couple of days later Millie and I are at the breakfast table and he's in his room getting dressed. All of a sudden he walks out, holding these pants away from his body as if they were diseased. 'Mom,' he says, 'did you iron these?' I told him to get back into his room and put those pants on.

"As he got older, he got worse.

"I think he was in junior high when I stopped by one afternoon to watch practice. I did that sometimes, when I got off early. He would have missed the bus, and I'd give him a ride home. Usually I'd be wearing a pair of slacks and a nice shirt, but that day I wore khakis. Clean, almost new khakis.

"That night, after we got home, he called me into his room. 'Dad,' he says, 'do you have to wear khaki pants to school? You usually look so nice, but those. . . .'

"I walked out of his room shaking my head."

I was continuing to separate myself from the guys I was playing with, athletically, moving to a new level. My last year in Little League—I think I was twelve—I batted .750, hit twenty home runs, and threw three no-hitters. But what really pleased me were those little signs of sophistication, like the pickoff move worked by pivoting my body and tossing to second instead of spinning around and throwing. That's much more efficient, and harder.

It was the same in football—I was developing a sense of what to do. My first year in junior high, I was playing safety one afternoon when I let the receiver get behind me. He was about to catch the pass for a touchdown—actually, he had caught the ball knee-high and was about to stride into the end zone—when I reached in and slapped the ball out of his hands. No one had taught me the move; it was pure instinct.

There was something else. To every game—whatever that game was—I brought a strong sense of determination. I learned that from my dad. I remember him coming up to me after a Little League game that our team had lost; I must have been eight. I couldn't stop crying. All he said was, "Did you do your best?" I said that I had. "Then I don't want to see you cry."

There were only two rules in our house: Finish what you start, and do your best. When your father's six-two and you're eight years old, you listen. It's like hearing the voice of God.

When I look at that now, I think immediately of the consecutive game streak, how many times that played back through my mind during those 1,207 games. My dad was always talking about leaving some mark in a positive way, something significant that could stand for a long time. But it was affecting me even then, long before I ever put on a Dodger uniform.

I went to a junior high school that had a tradition of good football. Just a few years before, the team had gone through a six-game schedule undefeated. All I could think of was how great it would be to go through the whole season not only undefeated but without being scored on. That became our goal.

The biggest threat to that streak came about midway through the season, when we faced a school with a huge halfback—six feet tall, close to 190 pounds, and fast. Because I was the smallest man in the secondary, they ran at me all night. Every time they tried it I got more aggressive, and more up, and they never did score. We beat them, 18–0, and never gave up a point that season. It's in the book. Oak Grove Junior High: 1962—unbeaten, untied, unscored on.

Being smaller than some of the other players never bothered me. (I was five-seven and about 165 pounds in high school.) I couldn't change it, so why worry about it? But I could work on being strong, so I did. From the time I was ten. I'd get those big Dodger bats—34, 35, 36 ounces—and I'd swing them just as I'd seen Gil Hodges do.

Later I started working with barbells. I had a set, and so did my friend across the street, Jimmy Markart. We'd work out together. We worked on our arms, but mostly we worked on leg strength—lots of squats and toe raises. When you start that young, and you keep it up, it pays. Through the years, one of my biggest assets has been the strength of my legs. Not so much for speed, but for avoiding injuries.

I got a lot more from the Markart family than physical conditioning. Jimmy's mother and father were my godparents, and they took their jobs seriously. Not that my parents aren't good Catholics. They are. We went to church, but not all that regularly. I hadn't been baptized or confirmed. I should have been by that time—I was fourteen or fifteen—but for whatever reason, it just didn't happen.

When the Markarts moved in across the street and Jimmy and I became friends, I started to go to church with them every Sunday. He was four years older than I—kind of a big brother I never had. I got along well with his father, Joe, who was a very decent person.

I was influenced by him, and by what I was hearing in church. I thought if my life is controlled by God, I should start to use my religion to get to know Him. I did. After a while I decided I wanted to be baptized and confirmed, and I began taking private catechism classes with Father Higgins at St. Lawrence, just a few blocks away.

The Right Reverend Lawrence Higgins, now monsignor of St. Lawrence Catholic Church in Tampa:

"It was unusual, to have someone come in at that age for individual lessons. But then Steve was an unusual student. He was very questioning. It was a conversation, back and forth. He questioned, he analyzed and then he would come back again.

"Even at that time he was a star, a teenage star, and that was important to him. But while he liked being in the limelight, he realized you needed guideposts to get through. We talked about that.

"But I don't think that was what brought him. Even at fifteen, he seemed to understand that he had been given special gifts from God, that he wasn't the only one responsible for his success. He appreciated that, and he wanted to return it in service. That is, of course, what we're all supposed to do."

My last two years at Chamberlain High were my most productive. I hit .472 as a junior, and, as a senior, .465, winning the county batting title and making all-city and all-conference for the third straight year.

The real test was during the summer, in American Legion ball. There the quality of the players was higher and more consistent. A lot of college athletes spend their summers playing Legion ball. I saw pitchers with good curves and live fastballs—pitches that had movement as well as speed. And while my average dropped to around .400 that summer, I was pleased.

There were signs that people were taking notice of me. First, there were college coaches; they started hanging around from my sophomore year on. Then there were the scouts—professional baseball scouts. With all the clubs training in the area—the Mets and Cardinals in St. Petersburg; the Reds in Tampa; the Phillies in Clearwater; just down the coast, Pittsburgh in Bradenton and Chicago in Sarasota—they were all over in the spring. Whenever one of us would see a scout, he'd let everybody else know.

After a while, you could spot them easily, sitting there with their notebooks, men with pretty good tans and wearing sunglasses. Invariably they had on old golf hats—you know, the round-brimmed golf hats, dilapidated from too many trips and too many games. Usually they sat in the same place: behind home plate, so they could judge the pitching, and a little bit off to one side, so they could judge the swings and the movement on the ball.

Theirs is probably the toughest job in all of baseball, spotting a player at age sixteen or seventeen and projecting what he's going to be at twenty-five or twenty-six. It's more than just evaluating talent. The best ones can recognize the personality of the player: how he's thinking and how tough he is. Those are the intangibles. They've got to do all this without too much conversation, because they're dealing with high school students. Just a few hellos, a few questions about height and weight and plans for college. Nothing more. From that they've got to make a decision.

It was nice to know they were there, watching. It put an edge on everything we did on the field, added a flavor of excitement. I knew they were watching me. But it had been drilled into me that I needed an education, and I was going to get it.

I had been approached by about twenty universities. The big Florida schools—Miami, Florida, and Florida State—and places like Auburn and Kansas, Wisconsin and Colgate. That year before I graduated I must have visited four or five campuses, but the one that impressed me most was Michigan State. There was an airline strike during the spring of 1966. I spent thirty-two hours on a bus to get to East Lansing, and at least that long getting back. It was worth it; I loved it.

I wanted a big school, and Michigan State had 43,000 students. And it was in the north. I was getting tired of south Florida, the heat and the thunderstorms. Michigan had real winters. Playing big-time football in a big stadium was also very attractive, and Michigan State was the only school offering me a full baseball scholarship that didn't object to my playing football too.

Years later I discovered that the reason I didn't get more offers was that coaches figured I would be turning pro within a year or so, and they didn't want to waste a scholarship.

At this time, actually, I was far from sure. In June, just before my high school graduation, the Minnesota Twins drafted me, but I didn't even consider their offer. True, it was for only about eleven or twelve thousand dollars, which wasn't enough money for me to take that kind of gamble. Had it been the Dodgers, I might have thought twice.

As it was, I didn't. It was set for East Lansing in the fall. My courses were all laid out, and so was my course. I was going to college to become a baseball coach and a teacher.

4

If you were selecting a university in 1967 with serious thoughts about becoming a baseball coach, Michigan State was a great choice. The reason was Danny Litwhiler, who was in charge of the baseball program there. Litwhiler had played eleven years in the major leagues, as an outfielder with Philadelphia, St. Louis, Boston, and Cincinnati. He remains today one of only four outfielders to play an entire season without making an error.

Not only could he play baseball, he could teach it. I had heard about him from before his Michigan State days, when he was the coach at Florida State, in Tallahassee. He had these "gimmicks," as he called them, designed to help players develop good habits. And they worked.

He had the MacGregor company make a catching glove without a pocket—completely flat. They called it the Litwhiler Fly Swatter. You had to use two hands, and it helped develop "soft hands," forcing you to give with the ball. To this day I catch with two hands.

He sawed off the top half of a bat to teach bunting. Whenever you bunt, the top half of the ball should meet the bottom half of the bat. Danny sawed off the top half of a bat, dramatizing the point. Unconsciously, you raised your bat and got on top of it, keeping you from popping the ball up. Casey Stengel used the bat; so did Fred Hutchinson and Al Lopez when they were managing.

Danny also developed the speed gun they use today to time pitchers. He invented an unbreakable mirror for pitchers to throw at; it let them see their motion as the batter does and showed them when they were tipping off their pitches.

There were other tools—weighted catcher's mitts to quicken reactions, multiple-direction batting cages for schools with limited space. He even invented a ball picker, a tube for picking up balls in the cage without having to bend down.

But what he did best was work with young athletes, teaching them the fundamentals to make them better ballplayers. That's what these gimmicks were—teaching aids. He was a master teacher. Under his guidance, I had a great freshman year. Until the injury.

My spring schedule was hectic. There were games on Mondays and Fridays, and double headers on Saturdays. I was also playing football, and spring practice was on Tuesday, Wednesday, and Thursday, with a scrimmage on Saturday afternoon.

Toward the end of May there was a big intersquad game. I was playing cornerback for the Green Team. I was about to tackle a halfback who was sweeping the end when my own linebacker leaped out, missed the runner, and crashed into my right shoulder, knocking me down. When I got up, my shoulder was numb.

I started to move it around, and the pain came. I couldn't lift my arm.

If it hadn't been such an important game, I might have come out, but positions were at stake for the opening of fall practice, so I kept playing. Two plays later I got hit by a pulling guard and knocked backward as the ball carrier started to cut inside. I hit the guy and held on with my right hand as he dragged me down the field.

Now I really hurt. They took me out of the game, and the doctor said the shoulder was separated, but not too badly. He said it would heal by itself, but he would bind it if I wanted. I told him I had more baseball to play that season, and he said to go ahead.

The next day I could swing a bat, but when I tried even to toss a ball, I had no strength. Using my wrist mostly, I could throw maybe ten, fifteen feet.

I missed a few games, but by the end of school I was throwing better. Not great, but better. My strength returned gradually, but accuracy continued to be a problem. From then on, it would always be.

It was sometime during that freshman year at Michigan State that my thinking about baseball and the future changed. My very first at-bat—I think it was against Eastern Michigan—after the opposing pitcher walked the first three batters, he started off with a ball to me. The next pitch I hit over the right field wall for a grand slam.

At some point after that I began to realize I was playing pretty successfully, and not against high school kids, but against guys I knew were going to be professionals. I was as good as most of them and a lot better than some.

Hitting .450 as a freshman, .435 over that summer while playing in a really good baseball league in Detroit and .383 as a sophomore, making all-conference and all-America: all these meant a lot to me. Suddenly I wasn't thinking at all about being coach—I was thinking only about being a professional baseball player. I *knew* I could be a good one.

Danny Litwhiler, former baseball coach at Florida State and Michigan State, now in semiretirement but working as a special instructor with the Cincinnati Reds:

"Steve was an awesome hitter in college. He hit towering home runs. But it was his mental toughness that was so impressive. He could accept the defeat of striking out. A lot of guys are struck out on a bad call and they're done for the day. It goes to their heads. He could strike out three times in a row, come up the fourth time and beat you. He never gave up.

"My only question about his making it was his defense. He didn't have the arm for left field. He had the speed and the judgment to play, but in the major leagues his arm wasn't strong enough. He was acceptable at third, but no more than that.

"It seems funny now, but I never dreamed of putting him at first base, I guess because of his height. You want a big target at first."

By the first week of June, when the draft was held, I was home in Tampa. I knew the Dodgers were interested in me; they'd scouted me. But they were picking 10th or 11th. You never know how long you're going to last, or whether they're going to find somebody else who fits their needs better. It just happened they had pitching and needed some power hitting.

The draft—the secondary phase, for players who were previously drafted but did not sign—was on Friday. I waited around the house all day, but nobody called. Saturday morning I opened the *Tampa Tribune,* and there it was: MAJORS PICK GARVEY, COOK. Tom Cook was a catcher from Sarasota.

I started to read the story, but who had drafted me wasn't in the first paragraph, so I skipped to the page with the full list of all the players. I ran my finger down the little type until I came to "Los Angeles—Steve Garvey, third baseman, Michigan State University, Tampa, Fla."

I couldn't believe it. It was like a dream.

The phone call came later that morning, congratulating me and saying that I would be contacted. The next week Guy Welman came to Tampa to talk with my parents and me. He was the Dodger scout who had been looking at me. I think he had seen me in two or three home games, and maybe one at Iowa.

We were all a little nervous the evening he arrived. Dad and I had talked about money—I think we figured anywhere around a thirty-five-thousand-dollar bonus would be good. Of course, because it was the Dodgers, I would take less money to sign.

Mom counted on his staying to dinner; she was making her famous stuffed pork chops. All of a sudden she looked up and said, "Welman. What if he's Jewish? He might not eat pork." So my dad ran out and bought some steaks, just in case.

This was a big day in the Garvey house.

Guy Welman, former minor-league catcher with Cincinnati and Brooklyn; for the last thirty-one years, a scout and coach for the Dodgers:

"A scout looks for different skills for different positions. For short-stop, second base, and center field, we're looking for good arms, good fielders, and good speed. We're not worried about power. Third base, first base, and the other two outfielders need all those tools plus power. Catchers should have power, too, but nowadays we're more concerned with defensive skills, especially a good throwing arm. We call these upper-level tools.

"*There are also the lower-level factors—the player's heart, how aggressive he is. Does he really want to be a baseball player? Judging, that's the hard part. But not with Steve Garvey. You watched him play, you knew he was aggressive. You knew he wanted it.*

"*I rated him as an outstanding hitter, with average running speed and below-average arm. But he had power to all fields, and that's hard to find. We feel we can teach someone to hit, but we can't teach power.*

"*Burt Wells, then Midwest regional scout, came to Michigan State's last game, at Iowa. Every decision is cross-checked. It was a double header, and Steve hit one home run over the right-field fence, one over the center-field fence, and one over the left-field fence. That got Burt's attention; Steve became our first pick.*

"*I flew to Tampa to sign him. Nothing had been said about dinner, so I ate this huge meal on the plane. Steve met me at the airport and took me home to an outstanding meal of stuffed pork chops. I ate till I was almost sick.*

"*Then I began my negotiations. We're supposed to pick out the parent we think is the boss and try to win him over. I figure it's Joe, so I'm working on him in the living room while Millie's doing the dishes in the kitchen.*

"*I'm giving Joe and Steve my best effort, working on their sentimental feelings for the Dodgers—I'd done my research—building up my offer. Finally I tell Steve, 'And I'm going to give you twenty-five thousand dollars and send you out as a Dodger!'*

"*With that I hear a voice from the kitchen saying, 'Mr. Welman, I will personally give Steve twenty-five thousand to go back to school.'*

"*Right then I knew who the boss was, and it wasn't Joe.*"

5

Welman had to call Al Campanis, the Dodger vice-president, to get clearance, but we finally settled on a package worth fifty thousand dollars—forty thousand in cash and another ten thousand to finish my education at Michigan State. Two weeks later I was off for Ogden, Utah, in the Pioneer League. They call it "A" classification, but it's really a rookie league.

I flew from Tampa to Salt Lake City, then caught a single-engine plane to Ogden, some twenty minutes away. It was about 2:30 or 3 o'clock in the afternoon when my cab reached the Ben Lomond Hotel, a big old relic downtown.

The sun was so bright outside that when I walked into the lobby I couldn't see a thing. But I could hear. There was laughing and chuckling, all around a central voice. It turned out to be Tom Lasorda, telling a story to a group of four or five players near the front desk. That was my first contact with pro base-ball—Lasorda's voice. In the many years that were to follow, I would have that experience over and over again: hearing Tom before seeing him.

For a rookie league team, Ogden was really something: Bobby Valentine and Bill Buckner, Tom Paciorek, and a pitcher named Sandy Vance. At the same time, over at Tri-City in the North-west League, were Joe Ferguson and Ron Cey; Davy Lopes was in Daytona Beach. All of us were signed by the Dodgers in 1968, and all of us would make it to the majors. The odds against that are staggering. That five of us should still be playing, eighteen years later, is unheard of. It just shows what great scouts the Dodgers had. The big club was struggling—after winning the pennant in '66, they fell below .500 in '67 and '68—and they really went after some young talent.

Your first year in pro ball is like no other. Everything is new; everything is exciting. You are a professional baseball player—paid to play baseball. This is what 90 percent of the boys in America dream of. You know you've got to produce, but you also feel, at least that early, that there's time. If you signed for any kind of a bonus, you feel they've got an investment in you, that they're going to give you every chance. That's the biggest thing—you've got a chance. Everything is still possible. It's a great feeling.

The stadium at Ogden was one of those old wooden types with wooden fences. It also had a few peculiarities. First, the dugouts were like bomb shelters; you could look up and see the fielders from the knees up. Then there was the field itself—somebody had laid it out wrong. The sun set in left centerfield instead of behind home. It caused a tremendous problem for the first couple of innings. A right-handed pitcher would be coming straight out of the sun. A couple of guys got hit; they could have been killed.

We lived at the Ben Lomond for sixty dollars a month—two dollars a day, home and away. When we were on the road they'd lock our stuff in the closet and rent the rooms to somebody else.

We got paid five hundred dollars a month, and three dollars a day meal money, which was spreading it pretty thin, but we made it work. There was this place called Chuck-o-rama or Chuck Wagon Buffet or something like that, where you could get all you could eat for $1.99. Salisbury steak, chicken, pork chops. It was a pregame ritual—everybody went, including Lasorda.

Of course we traveled by bus, everywhere. An old Greyhound with bad springs. Salt Lake City was the shortest trip, about forty-five minutes. Caldwell, Idaho, was the marathon: close to ten hours back to Ogden.

Early in the season we'd sing songs and listen to Tom tell baseball stories. It was lots of fun. As the season wore on and we wore down, there was less and less frivolity on the bus, and more and more sleeping. Some of the smaller guys would climb up in the luggage rack, but most of us would make do in the seats. They weren't all that comfortable, and every once in a while some six-four pitcher would get fed up with bending himself into a knot and stretch out on the floor. But that was like sleeping at low tide on a bad beach; you got awfully stinky down there.

The ballparks themselves weren't bad, though the lights were generally poor. The clubhouses were disaster areas. Minuscule— I mean, a fifth the size of what we'd had at Michigan State. When there were working showers and drains that drained, there was no hot water, and probably no soap. You had to be fast to make any of this matter; only the fast guys got towels. For twenty-five guys, maybe fifteen towels, and they were so thin you could read through them.

As for training facilities, it was good we were young and healthy. We had nothing. Lasorda's standard reply when some new kid would ask directions to the whirlpool was to tell him to stick his foot in the toilet and flush it.

None of it mattered, because we were young, and it was all fun in the purest sense of the word. Not only were we professional baseball players, but it was like you always dreamed it would be, a family. We played together and we ate together. We even killed time together. They had this bowling alley next to the Ramada Inn, and after games we'd all go over there. We'd have tournaments—Paciorek and I were one team; Lasorda and Buckner were another. Losers paid for the hamburgers afterward.

Lasorda played a big part in this—he was the head of our family, and he took a very parental role. He knew when to pat you on the back, and when to kick you in the pants. When guys got down, he would pump them up, telling them of all the money they were going to make in the majors.

We talked baseball all the time: situations, problems, conditions. It went on endlessly. And stories. Tom loved to tell stories. About where he played and what it was like. He pitched for the Dodgers for parts of two seasons—I think he started one game—but to hear him, you'd think he was the left-hander replaced in the rotation by Sandy Koufax.

Clearly, one of the keys to getting along with Lasorda was knowing *how* to listen to what he was saying. Sometimes it all got a little thick.

Thomas Charles Lasorda, sixteen years a pitcher, mostly in the minors; eight years a minor-league manager; and, since 1977, manager of the Dodgers:

"Steve Garvey was as fine a young man as I've ever seen in my life. He wasn't only a great ballplayer, he was just a tremendous young man, and it was a privilege for me to be associated with him.

"And in all the years I have known him—from Ogden to Spokane to the Dominican Republic to the Dodgers—he never changed an iota. He is still that same outstanding young man.

"I've made the statement that if I had a daughter who was old enough for him to date, if he were to come into the house to date my daughter, I would lock the door and I wouldn't let him out. That is the paramount compliment."

In many ways, Lasorda was the perfect manager for us. He was like a big, good-natured uncle. He knew baseball and he taught baseball, but he also understood the situation. Maybe that was even more important.

We were all such kids. Places like Idaho Falls and Salt Lake City were exotic. While some of us were in college, most had signed straight out of high school. But we all got along, and we all did a lot of growing up that first year.

We also played some pretty good baseball. We had to win three straight games at the end to win the championship, and we did it.

Buckner led the league in hitting with a .344 average. Paciorek hit .386, but they moved him to Bakersfield halfway through the season. Valentine was first with 62 runs scored and 20 stolen bases. I didn't do half bad, either, hitting .338 and leading the league with 20 home runs, 59 RBIs, and 151 total bases. I also led in errors for a third baseman, with 23. It wasn't my fielding—it was throwing. It was just a year after that shoulder separation, and I was still having trouble. I lifted weights and got my strength back, but it still wasn't working.

It seemed I made all the tough plays; any time I didn't have time to think, I was okay. Knock down the ball, pick it up, and throw the guy out. Bang, bang, bang. But if there was time, I'd throw the ball away.

As the season wore on, the problem wasn't getting any better. The following winter, when I was back at Michigan State, the Dodgers sent Guy Welman and Monty Basgall to work with me. Monty's been a coach and a scout with the Dodgers for thirteen years, and he's a great teacher. Together, they helped some, but throwing a baseball was to continue to plague me.

There was, however, something decisive that happened my junior year at East Lansing, and it had nothing to do with baseball. That was when I met Cynthia Truhan. (Actually, we had met the year before—when she was a freshman—but only casually.)

This was toward the end of the school year. I saw her one night sitting in the library, all by herself. She looked so lovely, studying there with her glasses on. Blond hair, those green eyes. I walked up to her and just started talking. Hi, how are you doing? How are your classes? Deep stuff. Then I told her I would be going off to Albuquerque soon, and I hoped she had a good summer. She said something like thank you.

During the summer, while I was playing at Albuquerque, I dropped her a letter, just to stay in touch. Of course I used my Dodger stationery.

I guess she was shocked to hear from me. Her father got the mail and asked her who she knew on the Dodgers. She said, "The Dodgers? I don't know anyone." She opened the letter and it was me. We started dating that fall.

She was different from anyone I had ever known. She was intelligent, and she had a kind of aggressiveness that I liked. Yet she was also very private. Cyndy was definitely a cut above. She had traveled a lot. Her father was in the military, and she'd lived in Hawaii and Kansas and Washington. There was a kind of worldliness about her, a sense that this woman could take care of business.

I was in love, for the first time in my life.

She helped me out at school my last year, arranging my classes, working with me in my studies. Then early in the summer of 1970, when the Dodgers sent me down to Spokane, she came to visit me. In July, when I went back up, she came to Los Angeles and I proposed. She accepted, and I was very happy. To be a Dodger and to be married to Cyndy—that seemed like the ultimate.

But all that came later. When I got to Albuquerque, a lot of guys from Ogden weren't there, a lot of guys who, when they had arrived in Ogden, figured they were on the way up.

There was this one big kid who had been a star in high school; he came in very cocky. He could throw hard, but straight. He could also be wild. He might start off an inning by striking somebody out; then he would give up a hit and a walk, and he might even hit somebody before striking out his next batter. So while he might strike out the side, he would give up three or four runs in the process.

Then they signed this kid from Chicago, a big, raw-boned Li'l Abner type, with black hair and a cowlick. He was a catcher who gave 100 percent, but he had no polish. He was strong, and once he got hold of the ball, he could knock it out of the park. But he needed to be taught catching. One time, with one out and runners on second and third, the pitcher struck out the batter and this kid rolled the ball back to the mound, like it was the third out. When the runner on third saw that he came charging home. That ended up being the winning run.

Lasorda went crazy. He was still screaming when the inning was over and the kid came into the dugout. "Hey," the boy said, "we all make mistakes." Lasorda told him that he was a professional now and couldn't afford those kinds of mistakes.

Neither of those guys made it to Double A, and there were a lot of others like them. Some were sent back to Ogden to try again; some went out to pursue new careers.

I had actually worked out with the Triple A Spokane team that spring at Vero, but I knew I wouldn't stick. I was on a break from Michigan State and would have to return to classes before starting the season. I didn't mind. I knew that sooner or later I would be in the majors.

Not everyone there in the Texas League was so confident. That second year is when you start feeling the heat. By then you've seen friends who have not been promoted, some who've even been sent back. And the worst—those who were released. It really makes you want to win, more than ever.

I remember once in Shreveport, Louisiana, the first time I ever played while Charlie Hough was pitching. Charlie had signed two years before me, but was having trouble getting to the majors. That was his second of three seasons at Albuquerque.

The leadoff batter that night was Angel Hermoso, who would later come up with Cleveland. Hermoso was fast and had burned Charlie before. To avoid getting caught with a bunt, Charlie told me to move in. I did. Charlie looked up before pitching, saw me even with the bag, and said, "Come on, this guy's going to lay one down." So I got in on the grass. Charlie's first pitch was a fastball in, and Angel hit a bullet off my chest. I picked it up and threw him out, but after the game I had this big red mark on my chest. I'll always remember Charlie Hough and Shreveport.

It was for Albuquerque that I first played first base. No technical decision was involved; it was because of a hamstring. In a game at Dallas-Fort Worth I had singled, and, while running down the line, I felt a twinge in my leg. I had never had anything like that before, so I didn't take it seriously.

The next guy hit the ball to center, and I took off. I got halfway to second when my hamstring went. It was like I'd been shot. I geared down, started hobbling, then fell on my face. The center fielder picked up the ball and forced me at second base while I was lying on the ground. They carried me off the field.

To get me back into the lineup—so I could hit—they put me at first.

Learning a new position is always interesting. At first base, the key is footwork—keeping your foot on the bag while reaching for low throws and high throws and wide throws. Certain plays, such as the pickoff and trying to gun down the runner at second on a bunt, are more difficult for a right-hander. Ideally, first base is a left-hander's position. Keith Hernandez, with his speed and strong arm, is a good example. Being six-one also helps.

The funny thing is, as a kid, I had always wanted to play first. Maybe it was the influence of my father—and Hodges. But you needed a specialized glove for first, and that was a deciding factor at the age of eight or ten.

For four days—that's all it was—it went well. You are off by yourself at third, but there's a lot of action at first, and that keeps you in the game. It's a very social position, and I liked that. I couldn't like it too much, though, because I knew where my ticket to the major leagues lay. The Dodgers had a gold glover at first—Wes Parker. They needed a third baseman.

I spent a good summer in Albuquerque. My fielding was still erratic—I'd make the great plays and mess up the easy ones, throwing the ball away—but I was hitting consistently. Out of 80 or so games, I had two hits in nearly every one—in 23 games I had three hits—and batted .373 for the season. Del Crandall was the manager, and we talked a lot about strategies—thinking the game, staying mentally involved every minute.

With two or three games to go in our season, they called me up to Los Angeles. September 1. That's the date the major-league teams can open their rosters and bring up minor-league players.

I had never seen Dodger Stadium before. I'd never been in Los Angeles. I was in awe. Sitting in that locker room, getting dressed, was an incredible feeling. The carpet. The bright lights. The stacks of fluffy towels. Just being there, in Dodger Stadium, as a Dodger—it was my boyhood dream come true. They gave me number 6, and that was exciting. It meant they thought I had potential, that I could make it. Not 37 or 49, but 6.

It was a Sunday. Thirty, maybe thirty-five, thousand people in the stands. Thinking back, there is a fog around that entire part of it; I was so involved.

We were playing the Mets, and they sent me in to pinch-hit against Jack DiLauro, a left-handed relief pitcher. I asked on the bench and they told me he had a couple of different pitches, breaking pitches. (Specialty pitches are tough, even when you know what to expect.) It was the bottom of the eighth inning, and we were losing. Walt Alston looked down the bench and called to me. "Okay, kid," he said, "go get 'em."

I remember they didn't have a helmet for me. I had to use a double-ear-flap helmet, which I thought set a great example for the kids but wasn't something I wanted to wear every day. Especially not that day. That day—that first at-bat—is so special.

If you ask any major-leaguer what is the greatest thrill in baseball, putting the ear foam on and going up there for the first time is right up there. That is the symbol of playing major-league baseball. All the preparation, from the time you're five or six, culminates with that first walk up to the plate. Sure, defense is part of the game—a crucial part—but at-bats are what stick in your mind . . . and in the record books.

I fouled off two pitches, took a ball, and then he threw me a screwball. I didn't know he had a screwball. I swung, missed it, and the bat came out of my hands and went over the third baseman's head and hit the grass in the outfield. When I came back to the dugout they said I had just set a stadium record. We all laughed.

The irony is that my last at-bat with the Dodgers was in San Francisco, the last day of the 1982 season. I had gotten up in the eighth with one on. On a 2 and 2 count, Greg Minton threw me a fastball, away. I still think it was a ball, but the umpire called it strike three. So it began and ended with a strikeout.

My second at-bat was against Atlanta; I flied out to right. But on September 10, against Denny Lemaster in the Astrodome, I got my first hit. He threw me a tailing fastball, and I hit it to right. Somebody came in to run for me, and when I reached the dugout, Ken Boyer was there and congratulated me.

6

There were several guys vying for the third base job in the spring of 1970, but I outright won it. I hit .350. I hit with power. I really came through.

As a sort of bonus, I got my first commercial.

Red Patterson, then public relations director for the Dodgers, came up to me about a week before the end of spring training and asked if I wanted to be in a commercial for the hair tonic Vitalis. I thought he was kidding, but he wasn't.

We were going to open the season against Cincinnati. The ad people were using Pete Rose, Maury Wills and me. We shot it during that off day before the season began.

The story line was very simple:

I lead off first base, then break for second on a steal attempt. As I slide in head-first, my helmet comes off, and Pete—still playing second at the time—tags me on the head. The umpire is Harry Wendelstadt, and he calls me safe. Then Pete says, "But Harry, look at the grease on my glove—I had him." Harry looks at the grease, calls me out, and I jog back to the dugout. Wills is waiting for me, and says, "Kid, if you want to make it in the big leagues, you gotta use the greaseless groomer." I just nod.

It was only later that I learned that if you have lines, you get more money. But I was pretty pleased. Shooting my first commercial—and a Vitalis commercial, the quintessential athlete's product—the day before starting at third base for the Dodgers! I was flying.

Then the season opened, and I did nothing. I mean nothing.

The Reds were tough that year. They had Rose and Tony Perez, Dave Concepcion, and Johnny Bench. With Gary Nolan and Jim Merritt, and that kid Wayne Simpson pitching, they won 102 games.

I think we got ten hits in that whole Cincinnati series—three or four games. By the end of April I was 5 for 32 and on the bench. Then they told me I was going down to Spokane. That very day I pinch-hit a double, but it was like the last gasp of a dying man. I was gone.

I was really disappointed. I had never been sent down before. I had never even tailed off. Nothing had really ever gone wrong. And I had been so high. I'd had a great spring. I'd been in my first commercial. I had been the starter on opening day—the new third baseman and the answer to the revolving door for the Dodgers at Dodger Stadium. I could hit for average; I could hit for power. And within a month I was being sent down.

Before I left for Spokane, I called my parents in Tampa. I said I've got bad news—I'm being sent down. It was tough to get it out. I was choked up because I felt I had let them down. I was embarrassed.

They were great. One and then the other said, hey, this isn't the end of the world. You're at the beginning of a long career, and this is just a delay along the way.

I didn't buy it easily. I told them I knew what they were saying, and I believed the same thing, but it was so hard to accept. I had heard of this happening, but I never expected it to happen to me. Since that time at Michigan State when I decided I was good enough to make it in the majors and set that as my goal, everything had gone just right. Till this.

Then my dad said, "Listen, we know you've given a hundred percent. You haven't let anybody down. Baseball's always been fun for you, so go down there and have fun. Everything is going to be fine."

I wasn't alone in Spokane. Buckner, who had also made the team and played opening day, had been sent down before me. Valentine and Paciorek were there, too. Not a bad group. We ended up winning the division by twenty-two games, then won the Pacific Coast League championship by beating Hawaii four straight.

During the season I was up for a couple of weeks while Bill Sudakis had to go to summer camp for the army, and I hit a little better. By the end of the season, when they brought me up again, I felt more comfortable. Hitting .300 in September brought me close to .270 for thirty-four games.

I opened up at third again in 1971, and wasn't doing too badly. Then in early June, I was batting against Mike Marshall in Montreal. He threw me a screwball inside, and I tried to check my swing. When I did, something happened. It was ten days before I knew just what.

I used to hold the bat down at the end, my left hand over the knob. That time batting against Marshall, in trying to stop the head of the bat, I dug the knob into the palm of my hand. I knew something was wrong—there was a numbness in my hand. But you sometimes get things like that. I shook it off and finished my time at bat. The next time up I couldn't lift the bat out of the rack; I knew I was in trouble.

Nobody could find the problem. If I let the hand alone, it felt fine. But if I tried to use it, applied the slightest pressure, I was in agony; swing a bat, catch a ball—any of the things you have to do in this business. They took X ray after X ray and found nothing.

We went into New York. It was the first time I had been there as a Dodger, and I went to dinner at my uncle's house in Uniondale, Long Island. The whole Ferraro family was there: Uncle Mike, Aunt Marion, my cousins. I asked for the ketchup, and when they passed me the bottle I almost dropped it. And then I couldn't unscrew the top. There was no strength in my hand.

Back in Los Angeles the team sent me to see Dr. Frank Jobe. He took a different kind of X ray, what they call a carpal tunnel view, taken with my wrist bent back and my hand held at an angle. It showed a break in the hamate, a little bone in the center of the palm. By 7 o'clock that night I was in the hospital, being operated on. I was out nearly five weeks.

Even after I came off the disabled list, I couldn't hit. I had no snap in the bat. But it wasn't a wasted season. I learned a lot about baseball in 1971.

That was an interesting club, heavy with veterans, but with a liberal sprinkling of young players. Wes Parker was at first; Jim Lefebvre at second, with a little help from Bill Russell; Maury Wills was still the shortstop. Buckner was back up and playing in left field, with Willie Davis in center and Willie Crawford in right.

Nobody was set at third. Valentine played some, I played some, Billy Grabarkowitz a little, and Richie Allen too.

Allen was with the Dodgers just that one year, but he made a real contribution, to the team and to me. He played at third, first, and in the outfield; hit almost .300; and knocked in 90 or 100 runs. He loved to talk about hitting, and when he talked, I listened. I listened on the bench. I listened on planes and in hotels.

He talked about how crucial the position of your body is to balance and stride. He talked about approach to the ball and going with it, pulling it, hitting it up the middle. He was one of the great up-the-middle hitters.

I learned a lot from Maury Wills, too. Mostly about the mental aspects of the game—the thinking game.

Maury was the first person who articulated to me the theory of never getting too high or too low. If you have a good game, enjoy it, have a good time, but keep control of your emotions. You've got to get down to that medial level for the next game. And if you've had a bad game, work to bring that emotional level up. You've got to maintain a controlled level of aggressiveness all the time. Not just from game to game, but from inning to inning and play to play.

This is not simply a philosophy of internal environment—keeping yourself under control so you can perform. Showing your emotion gives the opposition an edge. If they see you are down, it gives them a psychological edge. Your weakness makes them stronger. Showing them you are too excited is just as serious.

I look for the signs all the time. If the third baseman has just hit a home run in the top of the inning and I'm up in the bottom, I look to see if he's still celebrating there at third. If he is, I might just lay down a bunt.

So enjoy your moment of glory, but get yourself back to that medial level emotionally as soon as possible. Never show the opposition you're too high or too low. Baseball's a lot like poker.

Wills also liked to talk about the various situations for bunting, for hitting and running. Defensively, he talked about the best times to try a pickoff play, and little trick plays, such as dropping a bunt that's been popped up so you can make a force-out at second and possibly get the faster man off the bases, or maybe start a double play.

What the Dodgers were operating in 1971 was a graduate-level class in baseball. Call it Conversations on the Mental Game. The baseball knowledge that veteran players had developed over the length of their careers was quietly and informally being passed on to younger players. This wasn't a project of the coaching staff; it was the passing on of a legacy. The Willses and the Allens—they had it all to give for the asking.

On the field for me, there was one shining moment. Actually, it was my first in the big leagues.

My cast had come off around the time of the All-Star Game, and toward the end of July I came off the inactive list. I think I pinch-hit once, then started a game in Los Angeles against the Reds, making three errors and getting three hits.

Two days later we were in San Francisco, desperately trying to catch the Giants. But we weren't doing very well, and this day we entered the ninth inning trailing 4–2.

Steve Hamilton was pitching for the Giants, and I came up with two on and two out. Charlie Fox, then the Giant manager, went to the mound for a conversation. He decided to leave Hamilton in, and I hit a home run over the left field fence to win the game, 5–4. I can still see Willie Mays climbing the fence trying to catch it.

We did make a run at the Giants in September, going 13–2 in one stretch and taking a two-game series at Candlestick to pull within one game, but that was as close as we were to get.

Cyndy and I were married on October 29, in Grosse Pointe, Michigan. That's where her parents lived. It was a big wedding—two, three hundred people. We went to Caneel Bay on St. John for our honeymoon, then topped that off with a weekend in Montreal.

I'm sure I didn't think of it then, but an island in the Caribbean was a symbolic choice. Our honeymoon—our getting married—was an island of happiness in the sea of turbulence that were those first few years with the Dodgers. The beginning had been rough, and it was going to get rougher.

Billy Grabarkowitz opened the 1972 season at third, but it was clear the Dodgers didn't know who they wanted to play there. I ended up playing eighty-five games at third, but that didn't indicate anything like a decision on the club's part.

It was frustrating. I would play there for four or five days, and do pretty well. Then I'd have a couple of rocky days, and I'd be on the bench. They would bring Valentine in for a game or two, or Grabarkowitz or Lefebvre. Wills even played a couple dozen games there. At some point in the season, they brought up Ron Cey from Albuquerque.

The situation was beginning to work on me psychologically. All my life as a ballplayer, in the late innings with the game on the line, I had wanted the ball hit to me so that I could end the game. You have to feel confident that you can make those plays.

In 1970, 1971 and especially 1972, I was making so many errors that I didn't want the ball to be hit to me. I didn't want the onus of the Dodgers losing a game because of an error that I made.

I became tentative—I was just stabbing at the ball. The best plays I had were the tough plays, where I had no time to think. A ball hit to my left—I'd dive, get up, and throw the guy out. A chopped ball coming in—I'd bare-hand it and throw the guy out. But the routine plays were the tough ones. I'd have enough time to think about throwing the ball away, and I would.

It wasn't just the weakness of my arm; somehow the weakness had gotten to my head. I had this arm I couldn't rely on, and it plagued me.

To this day I get criticized about my throwing—for not making a bunt play at second, or not trying to make a double play when there might be a chance. But I just know, on the days when my arm's not that strong or it's not going to be that accurate, that I've got to play the percentages.

In 1972 I made twenty-eight errors, mostly on throws. That led the league and was the worst season of my life. But I worked—I really worked to make it better. Having coaches like Monty Basgall around was a big help.

All through that time, Monty worked with my fielding—keeping my knees bent for better fielding balance, positioning myself in front of the ball, using my free hand, keeping it ready in case there's a bad hop.

But of course what we worked on most was throwing the baseball.

Monty Basgall, a minor-league infielder for fourteen seasons and a major-leaguer for only two hundred games, mostly in Pittsburgh's organization:

"I was impressed with his fielding. He had outstanding hands, but he threw the ball like someone would throw a football, or like a pitcher throwing a slider, which is not the way you want to go to first base.

"I worked with him on his throwing, and got him to drop down a little—not throw so much overhand but come more from the side. That helped his accuracy. He was a good student; he listened, and he tried whatever I suggested.

"When a guy hits as well as he did, you've just got to get him into the lineup. We talked about moving him. We talked of the outfield, and later on we tried him in the outfield. I thought about trying him at second; somebody else thought he should try first.

"If I had more time, I always felt, I could have helped him become a really good third baseman. But he was already in the majors, and they wanted his power in the lineup soon.

"Time was they'd take however long was necessary in the minor leagues to work problems out, but no more. Now they rush them along so fast, and if there is a problem they just move them to a new position."

Improvement did not come quickly, and I could feel the Dodgers becoming impatient. Then midway through the season I began hearing rumors about my possibly being traded to Montreal. I tried to be philosophical. I figured, if it was going to happen it would; if it didn't, that meant they still thought I had potential.

When I spoke with Al Campanis, he assured me the feeling was that I could still help the team. He said he realized it had been tough for me, but that I was making progress offensively and that my fielding was coming along. He didn't exactly put my mind at ease. He told me, I suppose, what I already knew. I was still there; I still had a chance. But I was no longer a rookie. I had to prove myself.

One thing was for sure—I would have to play winter ball. All my off-seasons before 1972 were committed to Michigan State. The Dodgers had wanted me to go to instructional league in Arizona the winter before, but I had insisted on returning to East Lansing and completing my studies, which was what I did.

Cyndy and I spent the winter of 1972 in Santo Domingo. There were sacrifices, but it was an experience not easily forgotten. I remember coming home from a game one night to find her stirring a bunch of clothes in the bathtub with a nine iron. Among the things we did not have was a washing machine.

But we had a lot of fun, too. We had two rooms in the Hotel Jaragua, and they opened out onto the Caribbean. At night we fell asleep to the sound of the tide against the shore.

And the baseball was terrific. Lasorda was our manager. Paciorek was there; Valentine, too. We won our division, went on to the Caribbean World Series in Venezuela, and won that too. I hit around .335 and made the Caribbean all-star team at third.

It was a real lift for me, just what I needed to get myself back on track. Sometime during that winter, I thought of what my father had said in 1970 when the Dodgers sent me down to Triple A. "Just go down there and have fun. You'll be all right." That was what I did in Santo Domingo. And it worked. It got me back to the baseball I had known.

When I got to Vero Beach that spring, I found that not only were the Dodgers looking seriously at Ron Cey at third, but they had traded for Ken McMullen, a third baseman with the Angels. McMullen had originally signed with the Dodgers out of high school, but was traded first to the Washington Senators and then the Angels before making his way back to L.A.

Basically, that left me out in the cold. They said they wanted me to play left field, but Manny Mota was playing left, and if anybody was going to back him up it would be Paciorek. Somebody mentioned first base, but Wes Parker had just retired and Buckner was playing first.

I felt terrible. I could feel it slipping away, and there was nothing I could do. Third base had been mine, and I lost it. Ron Cey had always been behind me. He was resentful because I was always one step ahead of him in the organization. So now he would get his chance. McMullen would start at third, but they were definitely looking at Ron for the future. Which left me in limbo.

For a while I was down. I started to think of all those guys who had gone off with such promise, and then vanished. I thought of David Kent, a good friend from Tampa who went to Hillsborough High, our chief rival. He was a pitcher, who also played infield and outfield. Big, strong kid, six-two, 200 pounds. All the promise in the world. Signed with the Yankees and just never made it. Nobody could understand.

Even Bobby Valentine, who everybody thought had "star" written all over him. Great stats in the minors; player of the year in the Pacific Coast League in 1970. Then somebody in the Dodger organization must have decided he wasn't going to be a star, and they traded him to California in the McMullen deal.

I told myself, If you stay down you're going to lose out. You can't let that happen. I knew I could hit. If nothing else, I could hit the ball.

Then one night I got a chance to pinch-hit, and I came through. It happened again, and I got another hit. All of a sudden I went from last man to Walt's number-one or number-two pinch hitter.

I started coming out every day for extra hitting, trying to keep myself ready to come in in the eighth and ninth innings when the pressure was on, and before long I was making a real contribution to the club. In thirty pinch-hit appearances, I hit .400.

The only problem was, that wasn't the way I wanted to do it. Important as that role is, I never saw myself as a pinch hitter, a utility player, a part-time performer. There is a place in baseball for these kind of men. Jay Johnstone, Kurt Bevacqua—they've made a place for themselves, and make decent livings. But that wasn't supposed to be me.

On the other hand, I knew that 1973 was a decisive year. I was going to have to show them that I could be a major-leaguer. At third base or not. Even if it wasn't in Los Angeles.

I know that sounds very pragmatic, but that is how I look at things. That is how I keep the pressure at a minimum, so that it doesn't totally consume my life and make it impossible to function. I try to break issues down to basic components. That's one aid. The other is religion. In times of need I go to church and ask for help. You can do it anywhere, but there is something about the atmosphere of a church that allows you to concentrate on communicating. I spent a lot of time asking for guidance as to whether this was truly the right way for me to go. I also reinforced my belief that my life was in God's hands, to do whatever with.

Still, I was having trouble remaining positive. Time was pressure. I knew if things didn't work out soon I would have one, maybe two more years in major-league baseball. Then I would have to go get on with whatever would be the rest of my life.

Cyndy was very helpful during that time. She would sit and listen patiently, then come back with something like, "You've never been a quitter. Don't start now."

Actually, it was Cyndy who helped turn it around.

We were playing a double header against the Reds late in June at Dodger Stadium. In the first game, I got a pinch hit to left field against Freddy Norman, the little left-hander from North Miami with the good screwball. We lost anyhow; the team was struggling.

Between games Cyndy called me at the clubhouse; I can't remember just why. Walter Alston was walking by and asked if I was talking to Cyndy. I told him yes, and he asked to say hello. He was always very fond of her. She knew that for three or four days Walt had been working me out at first base, and we had discussed the chances of my getting a start there someday. It was part of the ongoing process of seeking a place for me to play. Third base? Left field? First base?

While they were talking, she said, "Why don't you give him a chance at first base? You haven't got anything to lose."

I remember him being on the phone and kind of smiling at me. He told Cyndy that he'd have to see. He gave the phone back to me, and ten minutes later he told me I was starting. I went out and got two hits, and for seven days in a row I got two hits.

That was it. I was the Dodger first baseman.

7

Billy Buckner gracefully moved to left field, and I ended up playing seventy-six games at first base. My errors dropped from twenty-eight to seven, and my batting average rose from .269 to .306.

Looking back over that period from 1970 to the middle of 1973, I have a perspective now I didn't have at the time. Painful as the experience was, it resulted in a lot of character building.

Things had come pretty easily to me till then. I'm not saying I hadn't worked hard, or that I didn't appreciate what I had achieved. I truly think I did. But those years heightened that appreciation. Whatever chance there had been of my taking success for granted, it was gone.

There is also a strong possibility that my struggling was directly responsible for my excellent education as a young Dodger.

I don't know how receptive to advice I would have been if I had broken in as Rookie of the Year. But since I was hanging on by my fingernails, I became a very good student. I worked hard on my fielding and throwing, of course, but the goal there was simply survival. All along, there were classes in hitting; my instructors were some of the best in the game.

The man I worked with most in the beginning was Dixie Walker, who had just returned to the Dodgers as a coach when I joined the club in 1970. He was a tall, slender man in his sixties, from a little town in Georgia; he still spoke with a Southern accent.

Walker was the hard-hitting outfielder—his .357 in 1944 led the major leagues—who wasn't going to play on the same team with Jackie Robinson. He actually initiated a protest petition to block Robinson from joining the Dodgers, and when it became clear that Robinson was on his way, Walker asked to be traded.

Eventually he went to Pittsburgh, but he played with Robinson for that first season—1947—and while there was coolness between them, there was never any real trouble. Above all, Dixie was a gentleman. But he had also grown up in the South at a time when segregation was a way of life. New ways were not easy for him to accept back in the forties when he was already an adult.

He worked with me more than anybody, trying to get me to hit with authority to the opposite field—for me, to right field. I remember him saying it would be worth twenty-five points to my average and fifty thousand to my salary if I could get it down. The twenty-five points was probably true; he was a little light on the salary.

A lot of players didn't respond well to Dixie's instruction because he criticized a lot, but I didn't mind. He kept at me not to be lazy, to work on the ball that's pitched away, and to keep my hands up. And mostly, to work at hitting down on the ball.

From the time you are a kid, you hear the words "swing level." You do want the swing to be level, but only at the point of contact with the ball. But hitting is a circular science, in which the aim is to strike a spherical object with a cylindrical one. It's no wonder hitting a ball "squarely" is so difficult.

It helps to view the swing as if it were part of a working machine. The end of the bat forms an arc when it is swung; the axis is somewhere in the middle of your shoulders. You begin swinging down at the top of the arc, are level at the point of contact, and the follow-through is up.

Start swinging level and you pop the ball up; hitting down keeps you from uppercutting the ball. You also create more backspin. It's backspin that carries the ball, gives it lift.

Dixie was with the club as a coach only through 1974, but that was the crucial period for me. And there were others passing through at the time, others who were equally generous with their knowledge.

I remember talking to Frank Robinson, who was with the team in 1972, about why he held the bat so flat. He said that eliminated any hitch in his swing and helped him generate more bat speed. Frank preached keeping the bat very still, which gave him more time to react to the pitch.

From Richie Allen I learned the value of a closed stance—keeping your front foot closer to the plate than the back foot. That gives you better balance, so you can pull the ball, hit up the middle, or go to right field. The closed stance gives you more options. With an open stance, it's harder to hit the outside pitch to the opposite field with authority.

Walter Alston always harped on me to keep my head in. "You're pulling your head out too much," he would say, over and over. To this day I probably keep my head on the ball as well as anybody.

I've heard guys say they keep their head in so long they actually see the ball hit the bat. I never have, and I'm not sure I believe they have, either. You'd end up hitting your head with the bat on the follow-through. But you do keep your eye on the ball until it's a couple of feet out. By then you know what's coming. A changeup has less spin on it. A split-finger fastball has an overspin. For a slider, the spinning seams of the ball form a dot. A curve ball has its own particular rotation. A knuckleball has hardly any rotation. An excellent knuckleball is so still you can actually see the label. If I can read the label, I'm in trouble. Knuckleballs are the hardest pitches for me to hit.

Pitchers do a lot of things to baseballs to get batters out. They put spit on them, or Vaseline; they rough up an area with sandpaper, or make a little cut; they'll take powder from their hands, and rub it on the ball—all to decrease the spin and have the ball sink rapidly, or run or slip inside or outside.

But to me, a well-thrown knuckleball is harder to hit than any of these illegal pitches, especially when it's thrown into the wind. I'm still trying to find somebody who'll teach me to hit Phil Niekro.

While Dixie Walker was a great hitter, he was a particular kind of hitter: great average, lots of doubles. He had a short stride, and he used to demonstrate it. He would raise his arms up high, like an old-time hitter, and then stride into the ball. "Step and glide," he would say. "Step and glide." But he had no real drive—he generated very little power. I think in his eighteen years in the major leagues only twice did he hit as many as ten home runs.

That's just not good enough. Power is important for me. I need drive; I need torque. I learned a lot about torque from Sadaharu Oh.

I spent some time with him during spring training in 1971, and then again in '75 and '79. He always talked about the use of his legs as the single biggest asset to his power. It was something I had always believed, and here was the most prolific home run hitter of all time reinforcing my own theory.

You've got to use your entire body to hit a ball effectively, not just your arms. That is the difference between a power hitter and a slap hitter. The action resembles a spring. You use your legs to coil your body, cocking your hips, lifting the front knee slightly. Then you pivot, striding into the ball, using your thighs and your hips as well as your arms to drive the ball. That's torque.

Oh exaggerated the motion, actually lifting his front leg in the cocking action, like Mel Ott. He made me realize I could cock my knee more than I was doing, increasing the amount of torque as I explode into the ball, using the legs as the driving force.

It was in those first years with the Dodgers that I collected all these pieces of information—leg drive from Oh, hitting down through the ball from Walker, body balance from Allen—and tried to incorporate them into my own style of hitting.

Throughout my career with Los Angeles, the man who most helped that effort was Manny Mota. All these men were truly knowledgeable baseball minds, and their theories were sound. I listened to them and accepted the merit of what they said. But getting their theories to work for me was another matter. Manny was always there to help. Long before he became the Dodgers' official batting coach—when he and I were both just players—he helped.

Manuel Geronimo Mota, who retired as a player in 1980 after nineteen years in the major leagues, the last eleven with Los Angeles: lifetime batting average, .304; total pinch hits, 150—the major-league record:

"From the very beginning Steve wanted to get better. He wanted to improve as a hitter, and he always worked toward that. Anyone who had something to help, he went there.

"At one time, when he first came up, he wanted to pull everything. I helped him realize that, strong as he was, he could go with the pitch and hit to all fields. Even in the major leagues, he could hit home runs to all fields.

"We also talked about situations. Before every game, we would sit down and discuss who he was supposed to face that night, what to look for from that pitcher. We talked about situations that might come up, and how to handle them. He worked very hard to be mentally prepared.

"Becoming a good hitter is a strange combination of being aggressive—not being afraid to swing the bat—and at the same time being disciplined and patient. It takes discipline to learn the strike zone and patience to wait on a pitch until that right moment.

"Steve learned that combination. That's why he is such a good hitter."

There was something else that happened about the same time. Not a big thing, but significant. I had been using the same bat for as long as I could remember. It was a Louisville Slugger, model S 2—a Vern Stephens. Stephens was a shortstop who played for St. Louis and Boston in the 1940s and early 1950s. He was about my size, even a little lighter, but he had real power. In 1949 he hit 39 home runs and knocked in 159 runs.

He used that bat, 35 inches, 35 ounces, natural-colored ash. The "S 2" designation was for his name and that he was the second player to take that model bat and have it slightly altered— tapering the handle, or whatever he had done to adjust it to his personal taste.

GARVEY

One night in Chicago, during the 1973 season, I happened to stop with some of the guys at Tommy O'Leary's for dinner. Tommy was a good sports fan, and he catered to a lot of the athletic crowd. On the wall I noticed a bat, a C 263—Norm Cash's bat. It was also 35 ounces and 35 inches—I like that combination—but it had a large head, tapering down to a narrow handle for the top hand and then flaring at the bottom, with a small knob. Ever since I broke the hamate bone in my left palm, I've tried to stay away from large knobs that would irritate it. The Cash bat felt just great, and I've been using that model ever since.

8

We came out of the blocks smoking in 1974. We took over first place in the Western Division on April 14, and by the first week in June we led the Reds by eight full games. But nobody was getting complacent. In 1972 the club was 11–4 early, held first as late as June, then collapsed and finished third, ten and a half games behind the Reds. In 1973 we had an eight-and-a-half-game lead midway through July, only to have Cincinnati get hot and take the division by three and a half.

I still remember a clubhouse meeting in St. Louis in August 1973, when the Reds were coming on and we were beginning to falter. Walt closed the door and laid us out. "It might be good for you guys to lose a few games," he said. "Take away some of that cockiness."

What he was really saying was that we were going out there as if we were the 1927 Yankees, but not doing some of the important little things. He wanted us to go back to basics, to execute better, and to stop thinking we were unbeatable. But the guys thought he didn't like their being confident, that he wanted them to be more humble.

Walt, then in his 20th season as Dodger manager, was not a great communicator, especially with young players. He was a quiet man; when he spoke, you were expected to listen. The rules were simple: hustle, take care of yourself, answer your coaches, and do what you're told. He figured we were all professionals, and nothing else was necessary. The truth is, a lot of us were pretty young.

It was an interesting meeting; we went down from there.

Nineteen seventy-four was different. We had learned from the past, and we were a better team. We had picked up Mike Marshall from Montreal. I had known Mike at Michigan State; he was a visiting lecturer in a kinesiology class I was taking. He rounded out a strong pitching staff headed by Don Sutton, Andy Messersmith, and, until he hurt his arm, Tommy John. We got Jimmy Wynn from Houston, and he had a great year in the outfield, along with Buckner and Willie Crawford.

I really think the key was that the infield had finally solidified. Ron Cey took over for Ken McMullen at third. Davey Lopes replaced Lee Lacy at second. Bill Russell had already taken over at short, and I moved to first. We would play together as a unit until the final out of the 1981 World Series.

I was having fun. By the first of June, I was hitting .338, fourth best in the league. My 47 RBIs led the league, and my 11 home runs were second.

About that time of the year, voting begins for the All-Star Game. I knew that, but it was nothing I had thought much about. Ballots for that year's game are made up from the previous season's performance. The eight slots for first baseman on the 1974 card were taken by men like Lee May, Willie McCovey, Tony Perez, and Billy Williams, all veteran All-Star performers. There was even a Dodger among them, Bill Buckner. I figured that was that.

Then a fellow from Los Angeles called me, Rick Allen. He said he was a fan, and that he wanted to generate write-in votes for me. There is a place on the bottom of the computer cards, three lines to write in players not listed above. He said he was sure he could deliver about 10,000 votes. I told him I couldn't authorize it, but if he wanted to, that would be terrific. I thanked him, and forgot about it.

It turned out that Allen published a television guide called "TV Facts," one of those pamphlets filled with advertising—I think they gave it away. He also proved to be as good as his word. A story in *The Sporting News* said that through the first week in June he had distributed something like seventy thousand ballots to potential Garvey voters.

The campaign got a lot of national attention. The press ate it up. Stories began popping up all over about the first baseman who was left off the ballot. And then the votes started coming in. The centers of activity, not surprisingly, were Florida, Michigan, and California—especially Southern California.

By the end of the month I had 280,000 votes, third behind Tony Perez. By the first week in July I had moved to second behind Perez, some 100,000 votes back. The game was on July 23, in Pittsburgh; balloting ended two weeks before.

The Tuesday before the game they announced the final count. I had edged Perez by twenty thousand votes. I was touched and more than a little excited. The All-Star Game! Twelve months before, I had been planning my teaching career; now I was starting at first base for the National League in the All-Star Game.

So what happens? The week before the game I woke up with my jowls all swollen. Nobody could figure out what it was. They thought it might have been impacted wisdom teeth, or maybe some kind of virus. All I could do was lie on the couch, drink liquids, and hope I was miraculously getting better.

That Friday, when it was clear I was not improving, Cyndy took me to the hospital. At first they said it was mumps, and that playing in the game was out of the question. They started me on antibiotics. Then Dr. Robert Woods, the team physician and the man in charge of my care, said it was only "almost the mumps." He said that an anti-mumps shot I'd taken a year before—something the whole team had taken—had weakened the infection.

On Monday I flew to Pittsburgh, looking very much like a chipmunk and feeling weak. I hadn't played in five days, and I was really looking forward to taking batting practice; I needed to work on my timing. But it was sprinkling—not even raining, just sprinkling—and that was enough to cancel batting practice.

At least we took infield, which I definitely needed. When I got out there, it was like I was walking on eggs. I hadn't exercised; I hadn't done any running. I was really unsteady. I knew I would be. While I was still in Los Angeles, I had considered staying home. But then I thought that a million people had written in my name. How could that not get me going?

The clubhouse before the game was intoxicating. The Reds had won the division the year before, and now here we were, battling them again for the pennant. And we're all in there, getting ready to play together. Perez and Joe Morgan and Rose and Bench, getting dressed beside Cey and Marshall and Jimmy Wynn. And Henry Aaron was there, and Larry Bowa, and Lou Brock and Don Kessinger. It was a thrill.

And the stuff—you can't imagine the stuff.

Adidas came in with white shoes, and they asked me if I'd like to wear a pair. I said, Sure, I'll wear white shoes. Hillerich &

Bradsby—the Louisville Slugger people—offered free bats, but Adirondak promised a set of golf clubs if you were named Most Valuable Player while using one of their bats, so I used theirs. And all the goodies in the lockers—the shirts and the shoes and the wristbands and T-shirts and warmups. It was like Christmas.

Yogi Berra was the manager, and he came over to me and told me that he knew I had been sick, and why didn't I try to go three innings, then he'd get somebody in for me. I said I thought that would be great.

The American League started Gaylord Perry, and he retired the first five men in order. I got up in the second inning with two out. He threw me a sinker, away. I swung, missed it completely, and almost fell on my face.

I stepped out of the box, looked up, and said, "Lord, please just let me hit the ball. Doesn't have to be a hit—just let me hit the ball. Don't let me look like a fool in front of all these people."

The next pitch was a slider. I hit it right up the middle for a single and scored on Cey's double. By then I was feeling a little better. I made a couple of good plays in the field—especially one against Bobby Murcer in the third—then doubled in the fourth against Luis Tiant, knocking in Bench.

In the fifth inning Yogi said he was going to get me out of the game, but he forgot. In the sixth he sent Perez up to pinch-hit for the pitcher, Ken Brett, George's older brother.

At the start of the seventh, Yogi came up to me and said, "Kid, I'm taking you out." I told him he couldn't; he didn't have any first basemen left. That was how I became the only National Leaguer to play the entire game.

After the game, on the field, Bowie Kuhn presented me with the Most Valuable Player trophy. They brought my father down from the stands, and he was standing right beside me. My mouth was full of cotton, all dry from the antibiotics and the lights and the excitement.

I looked up at the commissioner, who is six-five, and then at my father, who is six-two. I felt like a little kid in the middle of a dream. Then I looked out at the scoreboard, and read the words on the message board: MOST VALUABLE PLAYER 1974 ALL-STAR GAME NO. 6 STEVE GARVEY LOS ANGELES DODGERS. I felt my father's hand on my shoulder and heard the applause of the crowd that had stuck around, and I knew it was all real.

The club had built a ten-and-a-half-game lead by July, but staggered to the All-Star break. Tommy John, who was having his best year ever, ruptured a ligament in his pitching arm and was lost for the season—two seasons, actually. But we rallied after the break, and with Sutton having a great second half and Marshall coming out of the bullpen, all crises through the summer were manageable.

After two and a half very difficult years, and another of hopeful struggle, I was having a great time. Cyndy was pregnant with our first child, I was playing every day and doing well, and the whole team was getting a lot of attention on television and in the press.

It was during that season that I began getting more involved with the community in Los Angeles, making public-service announcements on radio and television for causes such as abused children, the heart association, and muscular dystrophy. I had thought about it before, but there wasn't a whole lot I could do. I was just another young ballplayer, without even a position. Nobody was interested in my name, much less my face. In my first years in Los Angeles I had made a few visits to hospitals to see sick children. Kids are so receptive; anybody in a baseball uniform cheers them up. I used to do that when I was in the minors. A baseball can do wonders, even if the child is desperately ill.

Once I began to get better known, I could have more effect. I had seen other athletes do it, and I liked the idea. It also made me feel awfully good.

That was how I got involved with multiple sclerosis. I didn't have anyone in my family with it, no close friends, but I was impressed with the efforts of the MS Society. I had been to a Champions vs. MS dinner, and I became educated that evening about the disease and the fight against it. It just seemed right for me. In their words, MS is "the crippler of young adults," a neurological disease that is progressively degenerative. In other words, it struck people my age and crippled them.

I had been looking for a charity to get involved with, to be able to focus my interest in the community in the off-season. And MS was one that used athletes—Billie Jean King, Muhammad Ali, Tom Seaver.

That next fall I put on a small tennis tournament. From scratch; I really didn't know what I was doing. A few celebrities, a few athletes—I think we raised three thousand dollars. Last year was our 10th. We raised close to $150,000 for the Society.

It was also in 1974 that I began developing my off-season business interests. That fall I began working for Pepsi-Cola. Not making ads or doing commercials, but doing marketing and public relations. Later I would do some cologne commercials, some print ads for Jockey, and then I got involved with the Allegretti Company. They make Paramount Weed Trimmers, the mechanisms in Weed-Eaters and a lot of other brands.

In so many areas, 1974 was a beginning. It was a good time for me and for Cyndy; it was a good time for the Dodgers. Everything seemed possible; everybody seemed happy.

Bill Buckner, who is now first baseman for the Boston Red Sox, was Garvey's teammate in Ogden, Albuquerque, and Spokane, and on the Dodgers till 1977:

"Steve was having a great season in 1974. We were all having good seasons, but with him it was different.

"He was always a little different. Look at how he dressed. Even in rookie league. Never a hair out of place. Pressed slacks; monogrammed shirts. In his locker, his uniforms hung in the same direction; all his shoes lined up.

"You just knew, right from the start, it was all going to work for him. He was a natural with the public; he always did the right thing at the right time, and the people took a liking to him. I don't think anybody was surprised when that turned into something commercial.

"People might think that being a good public relations man is easy, but it isn't. Making yourself available, signing all those autographs, always smiling. A lot of ballplayers don't want to do it, but he always has.

"Maybe everybody didn't think Steve could be their best friend, but nobody thought anything bad about him. He played hard on the field, and we were there to play.

"Personally, I had no problems with his success. When they gave him my position, I didn't mind; I like the outfield. When he went to the All-Star Game and I didn't, that was okay, too; he was having the better year.

"My only complaint goes back to when we first came up to the Dodgers. Steve took my favorite number—6. I always loved 6, and they gave it to Steve.

"It's taken me fourteen years to get on a ball club where I could wear Number 6."

Cincinnati stayed close through September, then won two games of a crucial weekend series in Los Angeles to pull within one and a half games. But that Sunday Sutton threw a six-hitter, Wynn and I hit back-to-back home runs—Jimmy's with the bases loaded—and we knew we were home free.

The season ended Wednesday night in Houston, and the play-offs began three days later on the road against Pittsburgh, the one team we'd really had trouble with. But the season is not the play-offs; you hear that a lot, and it's true.

We breezed through the first two games, then stumbled just a mite in the first game at Dodger Stadium. Willie Stargell drove in four runs and we lost, 7–0.

In the fourth game, Sutton gave up one run over seven innings and I went 4 for 5, driving in four runs. One of my two home runs was a line drive to right center that both outfielders were sure was going to ricochet off the wall. Jerry Reuss was pitching for the Pirates; he still can't believe it went out. The final score was 12–1.

We were ready for Oakland. I was named MVP for the play-offs, and I was starting to think: Wow, MVP for the All-Star Game, MVP for the playoffs. What can be next? MVP for the Series—why not?

I was ready. We *all* were ready!

So were the Athletics. They were twice World Champions by no accident. Ken Holtzman and Rollie Fingers gave up eleven hits between them in the first game, but only one earned run, and Catfish Hunter—of all people—came out of the bullpen in the ninth to close off the closest thing to a rally we mounted all day. They won, 3–2.

The great thing about the World Series is that it is a magnifying glass. Things become big, and the first game had a big play. A World Series play.

With one out in the eighth and Sal Bando on third, Reggie Jackson hit a fly to medium-deep right-center field. Wynn was camped under it, but Jimmy didn't have the greatest arm, so Joe Ferguson, who was playing right, cut in front of him, made the catch, and threw on a line to Steve Yeager at home plate to nail Bando. That throw would have gotten lost in June, but in the Series it won all the praise it deserved. People still talk about it.

Funny, but back in the locker room, I remember hearing Joe dismiss it. "Don't mean much if you don't win," he said. I guess we all felt some of that.

Sutton got us even in the second game. He shut down Oakland on five hits, walking two and striking out five. But in the ninth, leading 3–0, he got into trouble, hitting Bando, giving up an excuse-me double to Jackson.

Actually, he had barely survived the eighth. With one out and the bases loaded, Russell flagged a shot by Billy North, stepped on second for one, and bounced an off-balance throw to me for the double play.

In the ninth, when Sutton put the first two men on, Walt brought in Marshall. Mike gave up a single to Joe Rudi, scoring two, then struck out Gene Tenace. Alvin Dark replaced Rudi with Herb Washington, his designated runner and a former track star at Michigan State. Suddenly there was the Michigan State reunion: Marshall, Washington, and I had all been at East Lansing at the same time.

Marshall tossed to first, and Washington got back easily. Then he stepped off the pitching rubber and looked at Herb without throwing. He did that three times, never throwing, and each time Washington sauntered back more casually. But the next time Mike just pivoted and threw. I mean, I had the ball as Washington was just starting to lunge for the bag. Then Marshall struck out Angel Mangual, and we were even, going to Oakland.

Cyndy was back in Los Angeles, expecting our first child. And on the afternoon of the fourth game, with her in Valley Presbyterian Hospital and me at the Oakland Coliseum taking batting practice, she gave birth to our daughter Krisha Lee—6 pounds, 13½ ounces.

Nothing so positive was coming from the Dodger efforts. We just seemed unable to transport that momentum from the second game up the coast. The three games were tight—we fought hard—but we never got on the right track. I think we led only once, briefly, in that fourth game. It was over very quickly, and I was very disappointed.

It wasn't as if we lost to a second-rate team. They were the world champions—now three times running. Nobody had done that since the Yankees put together that incredible streak in the early 1950s. These guys had talent and they had experience. Hunter and Fingers, Reggie and Rudi and Sal Bando and Billy North—that's some team. They battled among themselves, but they had good talent and good chemistry.

That was no consolation. After the last game I sat on the towel table at the end of the locker room, numb. I couldn't believe that we had been eliminated like that. Not going six—you want to go at least six, at least win a couple of games.

I felt terrible. We had worked so hard to get there, to get a chance to win, and then we'd lost. That kind of thing affects you more when you're young than it does later on. Now I've been in five World Series, so I have some perspective. But when you're playing in your first Series you don't know if you are ever going to make it back again. That was it. That was what you'd been waiting for—dreaming of—the World Series. And you lost.

To be honest, as I sat there, I felt disappointed for myself. If we'd won, I would have had a good chance for MVP, which would have meant a sweep of that award for the three big events of the season—All-Star Game, playoffs, and World Series. You don't get a chance at that very often.

But that is the difference between an individual sport and a team sport. As a member of a team, you can have a great year and still not win. And if you don't win, no matter how well you played, you feel terrible.

9

I could never have anticipated, early in the 1973 season, when I was fighting with the prospect of becoming a full-time pinch hitter, what 1974 was going to bring. For all the disappointment that I felt after that fifth game in Oakland, it was one fantastic year.

During the second half of the season, and throughout the playoffs and the Series, there were all kinds of newspaper articles conjuring up images of my riding in the Dodger bus as a kid, standing there in the well beside my father, and stories of my overcoming the perils of the minor leagues and my own weak arm to become an all-star.

That was just the first of what would follow during the off-season: features in *Sports Illustrated* and *Sport Magazine*, painting me as the symbol of the new hero in sports. There was also a trip back to Tampa for Steve Garvey Appreciation Night. I loved it.

Cyndy and I also got a chance that winter to relax and enjoy our new daughter. We also got a chance to enjoy ourselves. We traveled—I think we got to Hawaii twice—and generally got our batteries recharged after a very hectic season. I didn't have to go to winter ball, which was an important bonus from the season's success.

There were other bonuses. In November I was named Most Valuable Player in the league, something that probably meant as much to me as anything that happened. Runner-up in the voting was Lou Brock. That was the season that Lou broke Maury Wills' "untouchable" base-stealing mark of 104, by 14 steals. He also scored 105 runs, batted .306, and helped keep St. Louis in the divisional race till the last day. The final vote was relatively close, 270 to 233.

A lot of people felt Brock should have won. Lou was one of them. He was quoted as saying the vote was consistent with situations in the past, when Willie Stargell and Billy Williams were overlooked. What he meant, of course, was that the vote was racial, that black athletes get overlooked in favor of white athletes. I think that happens. Though the majority of MVPs in the National League since Jackie Robinson have been black, there have been only eight black winners in the American League. It's probably true that a black athlete has to do more than a white athlete to win the award.

There is no doubt, I think, that the people who give out awards and shape opinions—in other words, the print and television journalists—go out of their way to praise white success. Where it is lacking, the lack becomes a cause. They're always looking for "the great white hope" in boxing's heavyweight division, for the big white player to dominate the National Basketball Association.

This is sad, but I think it is true. Ignoring it won't make it go away.

If the vote for Most Valuable Player in the National League in 1974 reflected this bias, I don't know. I hope not. You could easily make a good case for either of us, or for my teammate Jimmy Wynn, for that matter. He had a heck of a season.

The matter is complicated by the lack of a clear definition of what makes an MVP. Is it the player who has the most spectacular accomplishment of the season, the player who has the best overall season, or the player who has the greatest effect on making his team a winner?

I opt for the latter. And I think that I did as much in 1974 to help my team win as any other player. I would like to think that the twenty-four men on the Baseball Writer's Committee felt the same way, and that was why they voted as they did. However, I was quite pleased when *The Sporting News* made Brock their Player of the Year in the National League. What he accomplished in 1974—for himself and his team—deserved to be marked in history.

It was particularly satisfying for me at the end of that season to earn a Gold Glove for my play at first base, especially after my troubles at third for two and a half years. There were some pretty cruel jokes making the rounds in Los Angeles when people thought I was going to be the Dodger third baseman for the next decade. One had season ticket holders behind first demanding that a net be erected for their protection.

I tried not to let the joking get to me, but my inconsistent play was another matter. That always bothered me. Throwing became such an emotional problem that it was affecting my entire game on the field. Then, once my reliance on throwing across the diamond was minimized, my other skills could take over. I enjoyed working to become a good first baseman, and I appreciated being recognized for it.

Fielding is a funny thing. You can't just look at errors, and if the number is low, deduce that the man is a good fielder. There have been some first basemen, highly rated statistically, who in reality were not very good. If you never get to a ball, you don't make an error. But you don't help your team that much either.

The success of a first baseman is determined by his fielding percentage when viewed with his total chances, and that viewed within the context of the success of his team. If the player averages 1,400 to 1,500 chances a year, and he only makes six errors, there is every possibility he's playing his position well. And if his team is successful—if his play contributes to a winning season—that is a further indication. A consistently winning team needs good defense.

It's a wonderful thing to sit and talk about hitting stats and fielding stats and pitching stats, and certainly they are a measure of an athlete's talent. But this is still a team sport. The ultimate measure is winning.

When I was with the Dodgers, people used to make a lot of cracks about our infield. Some criticized the way I played first— my reluctance to throw to second on a bunt—and others made me out to be a magician. They'd criticize the other guys' arms, saying that my digging balls out of the dirt was all that saved countless errors. Maybe they didn't have the greatest arms, but what few people knew was that throwing low was on instruction. When I was moved to first base, the coaches had a little meeting. "That's not Stretch McCovey at first," they told Cey and Russell and Lopes. "He's not six-five. If you're going to throw off the mark, throw low, not high."

So I got a reputation for digging balls out of the dirt, and they got a reputation for inaccurate arms. But individually, you look at the All-Star Game appearances for those players, and collectively, you add up the playoffs and World Series, and you know the defense was not weak.

No baseball team has that kind of success, season after season, with weak defense. And that, in the final analysis, is the measure of how good an infield we were. We won.

10

The first hint of trouble came early in 1975. We were all in Hawaii for the Superteams competition—the Steelers and the Vikings; the A's and the Dodgers; the Super Bowl teams and the World Series teams. We defeated Minnesota to become the first Superteams champions.

From time to time I got an uncomfortable feeling that the guys didn't want me in certain events. It sounds silly, like kids in the school yard, but that's what was happening. They kept choosing up sides, and I kept getting left out.

At first I thought it was only that I was in a lot of events, and they were spreading things around. But it kept happening, over and over. Events you think I'd be right for—like the canoe race: good size, good body type—ones I'd practiced for—like the obstacle course—I kept getting by-passed.

There was no one incident, nothing you would want to say something about at the time; you don't want to risk making more of it than exists.

During the five days, Cyndy and I received a lot of attention from ABC, the people who created the Superteams. We were getting interviewed more than the other couples, and I could tell that was causing trouble. There were signs of grumbling—low-key, but unmistakable.

That was also the first time someone called us the "Ken and Barbie of Baseball." At first it was cute, but it got old very quickly.

Still, there was nothing that really happened, nothing tangible. The games were fun. Hawaii was beautiful. Each man picked up about fourteen or fifteen thousand dollars, and that was good. I put the whole thing out of my mind. Spring training was coming at the end of the month, and we had unfinished business. This time we were going to go all the way.

There was a certain coolness among some of the players in Vero Beach, but we were all busy. The Dodger camp is one of the best organized in baseball, with some kind of training scheduled for nearly every minute.

We opened the season by dropping three to Cincinnati, then two weeks later swept four from them at Dodger Stadium. I went 5 for 6 in one of the games and felt great. Midway through May, we had opened up a five-and-a-half-game lead. Nobody was thinking anything but baseball.

Then the Reds got hot and won something like forty of their next fifty games. As we began to get buried by the Big Red Machine, the seams in our team harmony began to show. Then came the article.

It ran in the *San Bernadino Sun-Telegram* on June 15, 1975. Normally I would never have seen it, but someone sent it to me with a note. "Dear Steve, I thought that this would interest you."

It did.

The article, written by Betty Cuniberti, said in part:

Steve Garvey is kind, thoughtful, brave, loyal to God and his Dodgers, and helps other people in all ways.

That makes him different from most other people in all ways.

Steve Garvey, by self-design, is the most valuable man in the league and the most lonely man on his team.

"You want to know something," said one Dodger starter. "Steve Garvey doesn't have one friend on this team."

Last year's Most Valuable Player in the National League stands apart from the other Los Angeles Dodgers. He stands apart in an abstract sense—in that he is, perhaps, a superior ballplayer. And he stands apart in a literal sense—at the end of the dugout, alone, signing autographs.

Most of the accusations credited to players came from Cey and Lopes, but there were several attributed only to "a player." It was charged that my behavior was artificial, that whatever I did—signing autographs, taking pictures with fans—was an attempt to gain popularity, the ultimate goal being to make money.

The word that kept coming up was "phony."

Along the way, Cyndy was attacked for being party to my conspiracy of attention-grabbing; it was even charged that we used our daughter and dog as props.

I was hurt and I was angry. It hurt to read those charges coming from my teammates; it angered me to see all this in a newspaper. If somebody had a problem, he should have come out and told me. I couldn't believe they had done that in public.

Alston suggested we have a meeting and try and clear things up, give everyone a chance to say his piece. The next day we did, in the locker room before the game.

I got up and said that if anyone has problems with the way I conduct myself, let him tell me now, face to face, instead of going behind my back to the newspapers. Nobody stood up. Nobody said anything.

I asked them about the things that were said anonymously, but nobody would accept responsibility. It was not a long meeting, and not very satisfying.

Maybe I should have let it go, but I couldn't. I figured an open confrontation might be the wrong tactic, so afterward I approached each of the players quoted in the article, but that didn't resolve anything, either. Some said they had made a mistake, that they shouldn't have said it in the paper; one said that was how he felt, but refused to give any specific reasons.

Cyndy was crushed when she read it. For her part, she had always tried to be friendly to the other wives, though she didn't always fit in with all of them. I think she was more shocked for me, that my own teammates would criticize me like that. It's okay for the fans to do it, or sportswriters, but to hear that from your own teammates . . . you just don't air those problems in the press because it's counterproductive for the team.

I tried to keep it in perspective. Times were tough. After such a great 1974, we were expected to be even better in 1975. But we were floundering, and everybody was pointing a finger at everybody else. Success is supposed to be hard to handle when you're young, but failure is a lot harder.

There was a lot of tension around the clubhouse. And because we were losing, the reporters needed another story to cover. There were several articles on dissension, and all of them centered on me. DODGERS GIVING GARVEY THE COLD SHOULDER, that kind of stuff. Of course that made things worse.

I very much wanted to accept gracefully what was happening. If you're going to enjoy the riches when things are going well, the flip side is part of the same bargain. But I was having trouble. Some fundamental principles were involved.

Up to that point, I had always thought that if you are genuinely nice to people and you care and try to help them—if you try to be the best teammate you can—they're going to like you. And being liked was important to me. When I was growing up, the athletes I played with were my only brothers. They were part of my family.

I knew I was different from many of these guys, but I had always been different. In high school and in college, I was the square peg. At Michigan State, on our yearly road trip to Miami, when they tried to throw me in the pool—they always throw the rookies in the pool—I wouldn't let them. I didn't want to go in the pool with my clothes on. It didn't matter. None of it mattered. We were teammates. Playing hard together and winning were all that mattered.

That was why this development within the Dodgers was so painful. It was completely different from anything I had ever experienced. Finding out how these men felt about me was the low point of my life.

I began questioning myself. What had I done wrong? Was the formula by which I had lived my life all those years not going to work as a major-leaguer? Had my attitudes succeeded in creating an island for me to live on?

All those questions, all those doubts, stayed with me until, eventually, I came to the conclusion that this was less about personal rejection than about jealousy. Not professional jealousy. We were all having pretty good careers, though not every one was having a great season. Since so many of us had come up at the same time, it was easy to plot our progress. We were all making a firm place for ourselves, and would probably be playing together in Los Angeles for a long time.

No, the problem I'm talking about is popularity with the press and the fans. I was getting a lot more press, which resulted in my being more popular with the fans. A lot of my teammates resented me for that.

There is a media situation in Los Angeles that exists in no other place in the country except New York. There is so much television and radio coverage, so many urban and suburban newspapers, that a player who is just average gets much more attention than he might playing in another city. And the player with big numbers gets that much more.

It is a situation that has always existed in sports, and it throws a lot of things out of perspective. Think of the great outfielders in baseball through the mid-1950s and mid-1960s. The names that leap to mind are Willie Mays and Mickey Mantle, both great ballplayers, who played in New York and California.

But during that same period there were two outfielders who were as good, or at least very close: Henry Aaron and Frank Robinson. The first played in Milwaukee, and the other in Cincinnati. Until Aaron challenged Babe Ruth's home run mark, few people outside baseball thought of him as a great hitter. Robinson never did receive the attention he deserved.

This has always been true. Excellent ballplayers in Houston and Toronto, in Seattle and Minnesota and Cleveland, receive much less attention than those in New York and Los Angeles. And it is not only performance that builds legends, but publicity.

You take that intense coverage that exists in a city like Los Angeles, with seven major and twenty-eight suburban newspapers following the team, turn those reporters loose on twenty-five athletes for the eight months that are the entire baseball season, and you can imagine just how much exposure a player gets. And exposure often converts to popularity, which often translates to awards, which affects salary.

The simple truth is that I got a lot of exposure in those early years. Part of it was the good season I had in 1974, followed by good seasons in '75 and '76. But another part of it was that I was always accessible. Win or lose, I was always willing to talk to reporters. I thought it was part of my job. Some players were happy to talk when they won, but after booting a ground ball with the bases loaded in the ninth inning, they were gone.

Sportswriters are human; the guy who is there for them when things are tough is the guy they're going to go to most often. That happened to be me, which meant that I—and a lot of my ideas—ended up in the newspaper and on television.

Another big part of all this is timing. In the 1960s, the anti-hero was popular—the Joe Namaths, breaking the rules and going their own way. But in 1975 the country was already cranking up for the bicentennial. I would have been out of place trying to fit into the swinging-singles scene of the 1960s, but my wing-tipped shoes and conservative ideas—a national trend in the late forties and early fifties—were making a comeback in 1975. And with all the press I was getting, everybody knew what my ideas were. One magazine even pictured me with an apple pie sprouting American flags.

I can imagine what some of my teammates felt: that it was a conscious effort to create an image. They should have known better. Most of them knew me in the minors; I was no different in Los Angeles. All that autograph-signing and hand-shaking and cheek-kissing, that's how I am and have always been. I did it in Ogden, when nobody cared. I do it because I'm convinced it can make a difference. You sign a baseball for a kid and you've done something he's going to carry with him for years.

Some guys can't be bothered, but when I look into those little faces, I can't say no. I remember when I was a kid and ballplayers had time for me—it made me happy.

Not that it's always a wonderful experience. There are a lot of very rude people out there, and some of them are sports fans. They'll shove a piece of paper in my face and say, "Sign this," or grab at my arm when I'm trying to eat. I get irritated. Usually I'll sign, but I won't give them as much as I normally would—a little less enthusiasm. Sometimes I'll even give them a lesson in manners; that's come with the years.

There are also times when I just don't have it to give. I'm tired or I've struck out twice and hit into a double play, or maybe I have just smiled so much I feel like I'm going to have to put Vaseline on my teeth to keep that smile from cracking. But they are still there, all of them, wanting, wanting, wanting. So I click on automatic; I smile and I get through it.

Again, I do it because I believe it's important. It means much more to them than the effort takes me. Hospitals are the best example. Nobody enjoys visiting sick people. Especially sick kids. But you never know what it might mean.

During the summer of 1971, Cyndy and I visited a nine-year-old boy at Orthopedic Hospital in Los Angeles. He had been playing Little League and hurt his knee sliding into a base. When they examined him, they found cancer. Just before we got to the hospital, he had had his leg amputated above the knee.

His mother told me he was just coming out of it, and that his chances of recovering were not good. I think she said he had a 15 percent or 20 percent chance of living. She said he knew who I was, and that he was a big Dodger fan. His name was Ricky Williams.

I went into his room, sat down beside him and took his hand. He was so weak, so frail. At first there was no response, no recognition. I told him that I was pulling for him, that the whole team said hello, and that they were pulling for him to get well. I don't remember being particularly inspirational. But after a few minutes I could feel his little hand move; there was strength in it. Then he opened his eyes. He smiled. He managed a "Hi, Steve," and then slipped back again.

We spent some time with his mother outside his room, reassuring her. Most of those hospital visits are as much for the parents.

I promised her when Ricky was better I'd have them all out to the ballpark.

Ricky pulled through. They fitted him with an artificial leg, and he went on to play tennis, to ski—to teach handicapped skiing and become an active, productive person.

I'm not suggesting our visit made any difference, but I do think that when you're sick, when you're feeling alone and scared, getting some special attention can bring a little light to a dark situation. And sometimes that flicker of light at the right time helps a lot.

If you feel that way, it is very hard not to spend a little time in hospitals now and then. Because I am so convinced that it does help, I get an enormous lift from doing it. What I do ends up helping me.

In 1977 I was in the worst slump of my career. I was something like 3 for 50, and even those three hits weren't very impressive. As the end of August approached, I had maybe forty hits over the previous two months. I was a mess.

There came a game in Dodger Stadium on a Sunday. It was Nun's Day, against the St. Louis Cardinals, of course. (Now the Dodgers have Ball Day and Poster Day and T-Shirt Night, but back then they had a Nun's Day; I think the nuns got in for a dollar.) Steve Brener, the team publicist, came up to me before the game and said there was a young girl who was a big fan of mine in the stands. She was quadriplegic, and she had asked if I could come over and say hello. I said sure.

She was about eleven, very pretty, in a white dress and long blond hair, sitting in a wheelchair. Talk about heart-rending.

The situation was awkward. I was on the field and she was in the stands. But we talked for a few minutes. Her name was Annie Ruth, and she was a real Dodger fan.

She asked if I could get a hit for her, and I said I would try. I told her that it had been a struggle lately, but her coming out to the park on Nun's Day, both of us being Catholic, it might bring me luck. She smiled at that, a big bright smile. As I walked back to our dugout *I* couldn't help but smile.

Bob Forsch was the starting pitcher for St. Louis. I opened up with a double; followed that with a home run, another double, a grand slam in the seventh off Clay Carroll; and finished the afternoon with a third double. Five hits, five runs scored, five RBIs. The slump was over.

As the second home run sailed into the right field pavilion and I rounded first base, the fans stood and began cheering. They remained on their feet, cheering, as I rounded the bases. At home I pounced on the plate with both hands raised.

That's something I rarely do, but the sense of exhilaration I got from breaking through that horrendous slump was incredible. The fans just exploded, and I got all choked up. The chemistry created by the interaction of an athlete and the fans is almost mystical; that strangers in the stands can, by cheering, actually transmit their energy to the ballplayer and affect his performance. It's all connected, what you give to them and what they give to you.

Do I think Annie Ruth served as my good angel that day? I wouldn't go that far. I know that she charged me up. And I know that most of the time visiting with fans gives me as much as it gives them. Their smiles, their excitement—it lifts me.

I would like to have explained all this to my teammates who were so critical of me, but I never did. At least not to most of them. They didn't want to hear it. From their comments in the papers, I knew they figured it was all an attempt at good publicity, all a sham. But to me it isn't. These situations just keep happening to me, because I truly care about the fans—am truly warmed by my relationship with them.

Those were tough years for the Dodgers, especially in 1975 and 1976. That Cincinnati team may have been the best I ever saw.

They were unbeatable at that time, and there was very little good news to write about in Los Angeles. So the newspapers wrote about the dissension on the club.

While I had friends on the Dodgers, there was at that time nobody I hung around with. In truth, we were very different people, from different parts of the country and different backgrounds. And our interests were as different as our backgrounds. That's usually the way teams are. Sometimes conditions draw players closer together. In cities like Cincinnati and Pittsburgh, the players live in two or three areas and have more contact. In Los Angeles, we were spread all over.

But none of this made any difference as far as the sportswriters were concerned. They saw tension, and they wrote about tension. And why not? It was real. We all felt it. Ron Cey. Davey Lopes. Don Sutton. Andy Messersmith. Steve Yeager. And me. It wasn't very pleasant.

Second baseman David Earl Lopes, Garvey's teammate in Spokane in 1971 and on the Dodgers from 1972 through the World Series in 1981, was traded first to Oakland; he is now with the Chicago Cubs:

"Garv made an effort to be liked by everyone, and I think it was difficult for him to understand that some people just didn't like him. It may not be for anything he did to them; it may be the image he projected.

"It's very difficult for some people to believe he's for real, to say he has no ulterior motive for what he does, that he's doing things because he enjoys it, that he wants to help people.

"We all have our own way, and my way isn't his way. That should be okay. But people were misled. They thought everybody was supposed to do what Steve Garvey does. Because we're all Dodgers, we're all supposed to be doing that. They forgot we're twenty-five different individuals.

"Autographs were a problem. There are times, like when something has happened or I'm in a bad mood, when I'll say 'Ah, hell, I'm not signing a damn thing today.' I don't think Garv will ever do that. And just because you sign autographs and visit hospitals doesn't mean you are a better individual. It just means that you have different interests, have different motives.

"And believe me, Steve Garvey has his motives. He has everything charted out in his life, what he's going to do. Everything has a motive, I believe. He's doing certain things now for later on, for after baseball. He has been since day one.

"The problem was that he was presented as better than we were. The press did that; the organization did that.

"Nobody can question that Garv came to play, and that he gave 100 percent every single day, no matter how he felt. It was all the other stuff. It created a tension that never went away, that never eased. In 1977 and 1978, when we were winning, it was just as bad. It was difficult for a lot of us."

The tension may not have always been visible, but it was always there. There was always that one group of players, and I was always isolated from them. There were parties I wasn't invited to. On the road, I was pretty much left to go my own way.

In some ways, it was an expression of honesty. These were not guys I was trying to be best friends with. But again, I had always thought of teammates as *teammates;* that was the way the winning came most easily.

While I like to think that tension didn't take away from our play on the field, I can't help but believe that it did. Had no divisions existed, we all would have had more concentration and energy for hitting and fielding.

Though we won in 1977 and 1978, and again in 1981, I feel we won in spite of tension. Usually it was below the surface and under control. On one famous occasion, in 1978, it erupted.

It was the last week of August, and we were battling for the lead in the Western Division with San Francisco. We were on the road, in New York, when somebody showed me a *Los Angeles Times* article reporting on a piece that had run a few days before in *The Washington Post*. It was by Thomas Boswell, and it quoted Don Sutton. It was the same crap, all over again:

"This nation gets infatuated with a few names. All you hear on our team is Steve Garvey, all alone.

"Well, the best player on this team the last two years—and we all know it—is Reggie Smith. As Reggie goes, so goes us.

"Reggie doesn't go out and publicize himself. He doesn't smile at the right people or say the right things. He tells the truth, even if it sometimes alienates people. Reggie is not a façade, or a Madison Avenue image. He's a real person."

I remember thinking to myself, I've seen this happen before and I'm not going to let it happen again without saying something. Sutton was pitching that day, so I waited until the next day to approach him. I showed him the article and asked him if the quotes were accurate. He said they were, but that he wasn't "exactly" talking about me. I said of course he was.

Then he started talking about how perfect I think I am, and, somehow, Cyndy got into it. I told him to leave her out. We went around again, then he started talking again about Cyndy.

Exactly what happened in what order escapes me, but I think he started poking me in the chest, and then I picked him up and threw him into the locker next to Tommy John's. There was a lot of scrambling, scratching and rolling around on the floor. Dave Lopes, Reggie Smith, Bill Russell, and Rick Monday pulled us apart.

I ended up with scratches on my face and my eye red from where he stuck me with his thumb. I don't remember what happened to him. It was about the maddest I'd ever been.

GARVEY

Of course, it didn't end there. It never really ended, until, one by one, we all left the team. And not even then.

To this day, when hitting against Sutton, I don't like to get too comfortable at the plate.

11

When I think of my early years with the Dodgers, it is easy to permit that memory to become clouded. The situation in the clubhouse was that potent a force in my life at that time. And while we did go to the World Series in 1974, there was a lot of frustration during those first seasons. The Cincinnati Reds seemed to be everywhere. They won in 1972 by ten and a half games. They won in '73 by three and a half. They won in 1975 by twenty, and in '76 by ten.

But winning all the time is a child's concept, a fantasy played out in Little League and on sandlot fields. Once in the big leagues, one loses that youthful innocence fast. In its place I picked up some reality training, learning not only that in a season of 162 games, coping with defeat is an essential lesson, but also that you have to see between the wins and losses, spotting the little dramas that go into making up the game of baseball.

One of those dramas happened early in the 1975 season. I doubt many people noticed the beginning; everyone knows how it ended.

After the first twenty-three games, we held a three-game lead over San Diego and Cincinnati. The Padres were not considered to be a serious factor, but the Reds and Dodgers were midway through a decade of war. We had dropped three games to them in Cincinnati to open the season, and they came west halfway through April, when we proceeded to beat them four straight. One of those games was a classic, an eleven-inning scramble in which I went 5 for 5 and Jimmy Wynn scooted home with the winning run when Dan Driessen, their young first baseman, couldn't handle Willie Crawford's line shot.

Playing third base for the Reds was John Vukovich, a defensive specialist whom they had gotten from Milwaukee during the off-season. With such hitters as Bench, Rose, Perez, Morgan, and Ken Griffey in the lineup, they figured they could carry Vukovich's .170 batting average.

But the season wasn't going well for them, and by the middle of May we had opened up a five-and-a-half-game lead. It was about then—some thirty games into the season—that the Reds made a switch. It proved to be historic.

They asked Rose if he would move from left field—where he was an all-star—to third base, in order to make room for a tall, quiet kid named George Foster. Rose—who had already moved from second base to right field to left—agreed, and the Reds took off. They moved to within one and a half games by the first of June, and by the end of the month led the division by seven games. They finished the season twenty games ahead of Los Angeles, won the playoffs and took the first of two consecutive

World Series, the only National League team to do that since the 1921 and 1922 Giants.

I don't think John Vukovich ever played another game for the Reds after the switch. He was sent down to the minors, and eventually traded. He now is a respected coach for the Cubs.

George Foster, you may recall, went on to a healthy career as a power hitter. He now plays for the Mets, and earns upward of two million dollars a season.

Many of the most important dramas in baseball never make the headlines. One was played out daily beside me in the Dodger clubhouse. Whenever I think of those early years with Los Angeles, I think of Ken McMullen.

In the spring of 1973 at Vero Beach, my prospects were seriously hurt by the acquisition of McMullen, a tall, graceful third baseman whom the Dodgers had gotten from California. While Ken had played several positions in his eight years in the majors, third was what he played mostly, and he did that very well.

I had actually met him before, back in 1960 when he first came to spring training. He had been signed originally by the Dodgers right out of high school, for something like sixty thousand. I was still a bat boy when he came to his first camp. We met in Bradenton, Florida.

Ken opened at third base in '73, but two or three weeks into the season he suffered muscle spasms in his lower back. That took him out of the picture, and gave Ron Cey a chance. Ron took full advantage, and McMullen was left to fill in and pinch-hit.

Ken and his wife, Bobbi, had two children, and were expecting their third. Then, well into that season, they discovered that Bobbi had cancer.

During that season Ken and I lockered next to each other, and we would talk about how things were going. Occasionally, after the game, we'd go out for something to eat. There wasn't a lot of serious conversation; sometimes we didn't even mention Bobbi. Throughout that period McMullen set an example of a man in a real crisis, a man still able to maintain his dignity, his sense of humor, and his commitment to his profession, and, at the same time, do everything he possibly could for his wife.

It was a tough year. Even when his back was well enough for him to play, he was relegated to being a part-time player. At home he would be making trips to the doctor with Bobbi; on the road, he was always on the phone with her.

The baby was born in November—a healthy boy—and Bobbi seemed much better for a while. But then, right before Christmas, she got much worse.

I know it was hard for Ken to leave her and come to Vero Beach that spring. But just as his coming to camp the year before had put me in limbo, now he was the one without a position. He had to think of his family. He had to fight for what was left of his career.

A few days before the season opened, he got a call to return home.

Bobbie died April 8, 1974. That night Henry Aaron broke Babe Ruth's home run record of 714 by hitting a ball off the Dodgers' Al Downing into the bullpen of Atlanta's Fulton County Stadium. By game time we all had heard the news. If you see a picture of that historic home run, you might notice the Dodgers are wearing black armbands. They were for Bobbi.

Watching Ken McMullen, seeing what he was going through and the way he conducted himself, helped me put all the little skirmishes of my own life into some kind of order. Here I was, twenty-five years old, all of my energies focused on baseball and success, watching this thirty-two-year-old man, approaching the end of his career, dealing with something bigger than baseball or success.

My professional progress during those years, especially from the middle of 1973 on, was good. I was learning to field my new position—and earning Gold Gloves, the symbol of defensive excellence. And I was becoming a dependable hitter. From 1974 through 1976 I hit .312, .319, and .317, with two hundred hits each season, and averaged 95 RBIs and 88 runs scored.

At the end of that 1976 season I was in a pretty good position to negotiate my new contract. It wasn't something I had to do alone. Few athletes these days do. By then I, too, had an agent—Jerry Kapstein.

I had met Jerry in 1974, during the playoffs. He had contacted me, told me he was going to be in Pittsburgh during those two games there, and suggested we have dinner. And we did, on the off-day before the playoffs began.

I had heard about him from several ballplayers. At that time he represented Rollie Fingers and Don Baylor, and Dusty Baker, who was then with Atlanta. He had a reputation for integrity, and hard bargaining. After the World Series, when we finally got together to talk business, it was clear we saw many things in the same light.

Negotiations began two months after the 1976 season ended. (My old contract, also handled by Jerry, averaged $100,000 annually for two years.) Because of my special relationship with the Dodgers, this was not a conventional business discussion. I had already begun to do a lot of public relations work for the club, to the point where my name and the Dodgers were closely linked.

It was my feeling—our feeling, really—that I would play out my entire career in Los Angeles, so we were concerned not only with the amount of money but the length of time. We wanted a contract that reflected my position with the club.

Viewing those negotiations in the light of what would follow in 1982, the difference is incredible. One would never think they involved the same parties. In 1977 the timing was perfect. I was right in the middle of some very productive years. The Dodgers knew that. And they knew how popular I was with the fans. It was a storybook relationship between a ballplayer and a team. So the atmosphere was very friendly; all the principals were happy. The contract was $1.971 million for six seasons, which was the longest running and most lucrative ever entered into by the Dodgers.

I remember the statement given to the press by Al Campanis when it was all settled: "We are very happy and proud to have signed Steve to a long-term contract. Steve is, in my opinion, Mr. Consistency."

We thought we could have fought for more money, but money was not the only consideration. We were building a relationship. This was a good contract, offering solid security. At the time I was probably in the top ten in salaries, and very comfortable.

Of course, within three years I was no longer even in the top seventy-five, but that is another chapter.

12

Even before the 1977 season began, we knew it was going to be a different kind of ball club. After twenty-three seasons as manager of the Dodgers, Walter Alston had retired. Tom Lasorda replaced him.

It was a big change in many ways; after so long, it seemed dramatic. But I think it was time. Walt was beginning to show his age, and it was becoming tougher for him to tolerate some of the individuality that was coming into vogue. He wasn't getting obedience from the players, especially the younger ones, those who had come up through our minor-league system and played for Tom. They had grown up in a different environment. Tom dealt with players on more of an equal level. He's more emotional, too, a slap-you-on-the-back, hug-you-after-a-home-run type. The most anybody ever got from Walt was a handshake.

A lot of guys were pleased. Replacing Alston with Lasorda was a statement from the club that it was okay to be yourself. I don't want to say the change was a relief, but, for some of the younger players, it was as if they had just been told they could loosen their ties in church. And after losing two years in a row, the timing was good.

Walter Alston taught me patience and a professional attitude about baseball. He also taught me about respect. While he stayed with me during some rough times, I felt he never really gave me the chance I deserved at third base. Those first two and a half seasons, when I kept getting yanked in and out of the lineup, were frustrating. I felt, given time, that I could have made a good third baseman. Obviously he saw something else.

I was not going to question Walter Alston. I mean, he was the second guy off the plane when I was seven years of age, standing there beside my father, waiting for my first sight of a Dodger. You don't question the man who was the backbone of the Dodger image.

Questioning was something I did very little of back then. Even when Lasorda took over, there were questions I had, but I never quite got them out of my throat.

My place in the batting order was fourth. I had always hit fourth. That's where a .300 hitter with power belongs. Fourth, or maybe third. In spring training, Tom moved me to fifth, and put Cey in my spot.

Fifth is a less desirable place to hit. You don't have as good a hitter behind you, so you don't see as many good pitches. They are more likely to pitch around you; collecting walks is not why I'm here.

I was not a big fan of the move. I'm not sure why Tom did it. I don't know whether it was to motivate Cey, or simply to appease him. Either is a possibility. Tom knew he wasn't going to have any problem with me; I wasn't going to criticize him. We had this father/son kind of relationship, and there were times when he took advantage of it. That may be a hard position to defend, but it's how I saw the situation.

Implicit in hitting fifth is delivering more power, and Tom was asking me to do that. My home runs had dropped steadily from 21 in 1974 to 13 in 1976. He remembered my power from the minors, and he wanted to see more.

I could do that. The power was still there. I started taking the bat back a little farther, like a golfer hitting a drive. You take it back more, getting more arc and more bat-head speed. You sacrifice some accuracy, naturally, and some contact, but you hit more fly balls, with more backspin. You also make more outs.

But the team needed power. I ended up hitting twenty points less on my average, but I had thirty-three home runs—the most I've ever hit, before or since—and drove in 115. That was the year that four of us had thirty or more home runs—Cey, Reggie Smith, Dusty Baker and me.

We also won a lot of ballgames. Right from the beginning, we won. We won 22 of our first 26 games, and opened up a ten-and-a-half-game lead through the first week in May. Cey was the main catalyst. He batted .372 with 11 home runs and 38 RBIs over that stretch. Long before the All-Star break, the race was over.

That All-Star Game was very satisfying for me, especially in light of the difficulty I was having with some of my teammates. The 4,277,735 votes I received was the highest total ever recorded for a National League player. That same year in the American League, Rod Carew received twenty thousand votes more, which is the record in the majors.

The entire season was a steady team effort; our lead never dropped to less than eight games. Sutton, Rick Rhoden, and Tommy John gave us strong starting pitching; Charlie Hough and later Elias Sosa worked effectively out of the bullpen.

Both Smith and Baker had good seasons. I was particularly pleased to see Dusty come through. Moving over from Atlanta after the 1975 season, he suffered through a miserable 1976. But Lasorda told him the left field job was his, and he responded by batting .291 and hitting thirty home runs, the 30th coming on the last day of the regular season.

The playoffs opened against Philadelphia in Dodger Stadium. We fell behind, 5–1, before Cey hit a grand slam off Steve Carlton. Then they scored two in the ninth to win, 7–5.

In the second game, Sutton gave up nine hits but only one run, and Dusty hit our second grand slam in two days. But the gem of the playoffs came two days later, in Philadelphia.

The tempo was set in the second inning. We scored two runs in our half, the first on a disputed play at home. The Phillies and their fans seemed to think I never touched the plate, which is patently untrue.

They went ahead in their half when Burt Hooten walked three consecutive batters with the bases already loaded. We later tied it, but they went ahead with two in the bottom of the eighth. So the game came down to the ninth inning, with Philadelphia leading, 5–3.

With two out and nobody on, Tom sent in our geriatric pinch-hitting squad. Vic Davalillo, age 38, reclaimed late in the season from Aguascalientes in the Mexican League, dragged a bunt past the pitcher. Manny Mota, 39, lifted a high fly double off Greg Luzunski's glove in left, scoring Davalillo; Manny went to third on a bad throw to the infield. Lopes reached on another disputed call, took second on an errant pickoff, and scored on Russell's single up the middle.

It was a barn burner. It also took the steam out of the Phillies. In the final game, Tommy John gave up one run, and Baker hit a two-run homer to win the game and the playoffs.

The World Series was to start three days later in New York, and I was psyched. This was my fantasy—the Yankees against the Dodgers, and I was playing for the Dodgers. That's heady stuff.

A Dodger-Yankee pairing is the only type of World Series that gets the whole country involved. It's New York, it's Los Angeles—the two coasts and the two most traditional teams. It's the two most charismatic teams, with two exciting managers—Billy Martin and Tom Lasorda. George Steinbrenner is one owner and Walter O'Malley is the other; that's two ends of a spectrum.

The Yankees versus the Dodgers for nine days lights up the nation. It's the Kentucky Derby, the Indianapolis 500, the U.S. Open, and the Super Bowl all in one. To see it is a thrill, but to participate, well, you're talking about making history.

The first game was a testament to that, even though we lost. We tied it in the top of the ninth, but they won in the twelfth on a double by Willie Randolph and a single by Paul Blair, who had come over from Baltimore after thirteen seasons. He had only one hit in the Series, and he beat us with it.

One of the big plays in that game came in the sixth inning, when Nestor Chylak said that Thurman Munson had tagged me out at home. He was wrong. I was safe; Chylak was out of position and could not possibly have seen.

I'm generally not a screamer, but I got pretty hot on that call. Chylak was up the first base line, a good ten feet away from the play. I've never been thrown out of a ballgame, but the closest has been when the umpire has been out of position.

Mostly, I think they do a good job, especially under all that pressure. The travel is killing. And with more and more television, and video replays from different angles, they are constantly being second-guessed.

But baseball is a game played by human beings, and it has to be umpired by human beings. It is also a game that teaches humility. Errors are in the rule book because players misplay balls in the field. Even the best hitters make out two of every three attempts at the plate.

We won the second game as Cey, Yeager, and I hit line drives over the left field fence, and Smith put one into the right center field bleachers.

Unfortunately, that was the high point of our Series. New York took the first two games in Los Angeles, and, while we managed to win game five, back in New York Reggie Jackson's dramatic three-home-run barrage buried us.

Losing the Series didn't affect me the way it had in 1974. My perspective had changed. First, I no longer had any thought that this was a once-in-a-lifetime event. I knew we were going to be back, and I knew we were capable of winning. Also, L.A.–Oakland was one thing, and L.A.–New York was quite another. While I would so much have preferred to win, even losing was better than never having been there.

By 1977 I was beginning to be more active in the commercial arena. Some of it came through the William Morris Agency; some of it through Jerry Kapstein; and some through Abrams-Rubaloff, a commercial agency in Los Angeles and New York.

I had begun working for the Allegretti company early that year, doing print ads and radio spots for their various lawn-care products. That is a relationship that still exists, though it has become more personal than professional, extending to the Allegretti family. In many ways, they are in my adult years what the Markarts were in my teens—positive examples for me because of their strong commitment to Catholicism and their community involvement.

There were other projects. Cyndy and I did a Geritol commercial, and I did one for Aqua cologne. She did some modeling on
her own; we did some together. I did a print ad for Jockey, along
with Lou Brock, John Havlicek and several other athletes. There
was Swanson's Hungry Man Dinners, and a batting device for
kids made by Mattel.

All of this was just beginning to gain momentum that year.
Before long I was earning a sum equal to half my baseball salary
in off-the-field activities. By the time I left the Dodgers, I was
coming very close to equaling it.

At the same time, I was doing a lot of community work, especially with the MS Society. At first it was just the celebrity tennis
tournament, which did well from the start, and continued to
grow. About the third year it became a two-day event, and then I
added racquetball, and then a 10-kilometer run. We brought in
Pepsi as a sponsor and invited some top runners—Bill Rodgers,
Henry Rono, Rod Dixon.

Later there would come a number of golf tournaments, one for
the Oral Education Center in Los Angeles, which teaches deaf
children to speak, and another one in San Diego, the proceeds
going to a variety of charities.

Because of the friction with my teammates, any civic work I
did—at least for those years—raised questions of my motives. I
resented it, but I also learned from it. I thought more about what
I was doing. The result was a clearer understanding, for myself,
personally, of my actions.

You cannot walk into a stadium filled with fifty thousand people, hear them cheering, and not realize that this is a game that
exists because of their enthusiasm. We are not surgeons, or even
plumbers. Society cannot do without those skills; it can certainly
do without ballplayers. The fact that it does not exercise that

option is something for which I as a ballplayer am profoundly thankful.

Furthermore, that I am physically able to compete at the highest level of my game is a powerful reality to me. I may improve my performance by working hard, but God gave me the basic tools to be here in the first place. And because He did, I owe a debt. Spending time with the sick, and raising money for the infirm are two ways of paying that debt.

It is an attitude that became formalized back in Father Higgins' study in Tampa. "What God gives you in ability," he used to say, "you give back in service." In its own way, that's where the junior high school comes in.

It was toward the end of the 1977 season when I got a call from Bob Edwards, who introduced himself as the principal of Lindsay Junior High School. Lindsay, he explained, is a town of about 6,400 people in the central part of California's San Joaquin Valley, some two hundred miles north of Los Angeles. Farming is the industry, citrus the main product. What fame they have comes from the olives. He said they were in the process of renaming the school, and that I was one of three finalists. He wanted to know if I had any objections.

Obviously, this question had not come up before, and I wasn't quite sure what to say. I told him I would have to let him know.

The school was, from what I was told, in trouble. One report said it had become known for delinquent behavior among its students, for vandalism, rundown buildings and student apathy. Conditions were so bad, according to one newspaper article, that the school's official name, The Lincoln School, had been dropped. Most people just called it "the junior high."

One of the primary reasons, this article said, was the wide divergence of social classes within the town limits—middle and upper classes at one end; farm workers, most of whom were

Mexican-American, at the other. The friction often resulted in fights in the school yard.

"It was said around town that if you had business at the school," the article stated, "you were taking your life in your hands. It was dangerous just walking down the halls during recess."

Edwards said that he wasn't looking for money, just a fresh start for the school, a reason to clean up the graffiti. He wanted to boost the morale. I decided that was a good idea, something I would like to be a party to.

The first time we visited was in February 1978. Cyndy and I drove out one day in the middle of the week; we had to leave Los Angeles at 7:30 in the morning to meet the schedule. As we drove up to the front of the school, it was quite a scene. The school itself looked terrific. They had painted it, and planted new bushes. The new name, on a little brick wall all its own, stood right out: STEVE GARVEY JUNIOR HIGH SCHOOL.

It was quite a thrill. I've been back every February since, and it's still a thrill.

There's something wonderful about the energy that the students put into those visits. It's a special day: There's a greeting at the entrance; a press conference, where I meet with members of the student council; and the highlight of the day, the assembly, where the school band plays, the Spirit Squad performs, and the choir sings.

It really affects me—the whole day: from the reception committee to the pledge of the allegiance to the school lunch after the assembly, sitting on those straight-backed chairs and eating hamburgers and drinking milk. When you spend as much time in fancy hotels and on airplanes as I do, when you see so much attention paid to expensive clothes and flashy cars—when you find yourself doing the same thing—a scene like Lindsay is very refreshing.

Every year, when I leave, they give me boxes and boxes of the produce grown in the valley. Oranges and lemons and olives, and some fruit that is a mixture of an orange and a grapefruit. Not a box of each—two or three boxes of each; jars and jars of olives. I began bringing a larger car, just to get the stuff home.

I also come away with a sense that this relationship really means something to these kids. Not just the name on the school, but the continued association. I'm not quite sure what it is, but I have the sense that it is positive. I know it is for me.

When this whole thing started, back in 1977, I suggested to the principal that he use another athlete. Maybe Tom Seaver, who is from Fresno. Now I'm glad he didn't listen.

I got into an early groove in 1978, hitting safely in my first twenty-one games. We all started off pretty well, showing no ill effects from losing to the Yankees. Then, midway through May, we began to unravel. Our home run production, so healthy the season before, fell off, and our pitching was not so effective. Tommy John kept us close.

Toward the end of June we trailed San Francisco by six games, but that was to be the worst of it. Bob Welch came up from Albuquerque, and he helped, and by July we were back in the thick of it.

I had a good All-Star Game and was named Most Valuable Player for the second time, but I was not having a great summer. The tension in the clubhouse was getting to me, and I think it was affecting my hitting.

Then came the fight with Sutton. Four years of pressure erupted that night in New York. Afterward I went out against the Mets and got a couple of hits, and hit something like .430 for the rest of the season. We ended up winning by two and a half games and played the Phillies in the playoffs.

We won the first two games in Philadelphia, the second on a four-hit shutout by Tommy John, but lost to Carlton in the first game at Dodger Stadium. We won the next game, and the play-offs, by carving out a run in the tenth inning—a walk, an error by Garry Maddox, a single by Bill Russell, and we were home free.

The day after we wrapped up the playoffs, Jim Gilliam died. He had had a stroke, and died while we were getting ready to open the World Series.

My memories of Jim are vivid. When I first started as a bat boy, he was there. I remember him sitting on the steps of the dugout, his hat off, enjoying the sun. He would sit there during most of the game, chewing gum, watching the young guys on the field, watching the newest challenger out after his job.

Then in the last couple of innings, he would put on his hat, pick up his glove and go in there and play like it was the seventh game of the World Series. He'd hit the ball to all fields, steal a base, always be looking to take the extra base.

He had an attitude, an approach to the game, that impressed me even as a kid. When I signed with the Dodgers, he would work with me on my fielding and my hitting. We were very close. He used to call me Stevie. Not too many people called me Stevie by the time I was on the Dodgers; I was in my twenties then.

His funeral was the morning of the second game of the World Series. His wife asked me to be one of the pall bearers, along with Tom Lasorda, Don Newcombe, and some others I don't recall. It was a very emotional funeral. Jim Lefebvre spoke, but what I remember most was the Reverend Jesse Jackson. He gave the eulogy.

His theme was walking into a headwind. He said that Jim Gilliam, throughout his life, had always been challenged. Because of his race, he had trouble achieving his goals, that it was a constant struggle.

I could have misinterpreted this, but I don't think I did. And I don't think that Gilliam felt that way. Later, I heard someone say that Jackson had delivered the same eulogy at Jackie Robinson's funeral. That image of walking against the wind, that might be apt for some—probably it was for Jackie Robinson—but I don't think it fit Jim.

I remember clasping the handle of the casket and walking it out of the church; and then at the cemetery, placing it down. I felt sad, because I wanted there to be some kind of gesture praising Gilliam and how he had lived his life. The Dodgers wore black armbands, and that was nice, but it wasn't enough. They created the Jim Gilliam Memorial Award, and that was nice, too. But that wasn't the spirit of Jim Gilliam. He was a man who loved competition and loved the outdoors—especially golf. That was what we should have done, created the Jim Gilliam Golf Tournament. But we didn't.

We opened up strong against the Yankees at Dodger Stadium. The score was 6–0 before they managed to run in the top of the seventh. Tommy John weakened in that inning, and had to be relieved by Terry Forster in the eighth, but we breezed to an 11–5 win.

The second game was more exciting. Trailing 2–1 in the sixth inning, Cey hit a home run with two on.

New York came back with a run in the seventh, and things stayed at 4–3 Los Angeles as we rolled into the ninth. The Yankees had two men on with one away when Lasorda replaced Forester with Bob Welch, the big rookie. In the twenty-three games he'd relieved in since coming up, he had looked sharp—on occasion, overpowering.

Preschool graduation . . .
age five years. *Photo
courtesy Garvey family*

our house in
mpa, circa 1957.
*oto courtesy Garvey
nily*

Spring training—birth of a fantasy.
Photo courtesy Garvey family

On Chamberlain High's basketball
team, I played guard. *Chamberlain High
School Photo*

Playing defense for the Chiefs taught me tenacity. *Chamberlain High School Photo*

aring a Dodger uniform was a ill, even in Ogden, Utah. *Photo Mark Adrian*

Whenever Dixie Walker talked about hitting, I listened. *Photo by Newsday*

Casey Stengel was a prize interview at Old Timer's Day in 1974. © *1974 Los Angeles Dodgers, Inc.*

With my father and Commissioner Bowie Kuhn at All-Star Game. *AP/Wide World Photos*

Jimmy Wynn welcoming me after home run in pennant-winner against Pittsburgh in 1974. *AP/Wide World Photos*

Krisha at twenty-one months, visiting Dodger Stadium in 1976. *Photo by Mark Malone*

Whitney, at one year, evaluates bat during 1977 Family Day. *UPI/Bettmann Newsphotos*

Dodger 30-Home Run Club of 1977: Ron Cey and Dusty Baker kneeling, Reggie Smith and I standing. © *1977 Los Angeles Dodgers, Inc.*

elebrating with Tom
asorda after pennant win
er Philadelphia in 1977.
hoto by Bob Bartosz

Sock hop during an early
visit to Garvey Junior High.
Lindsay Gazette Photo

In Lindsay last year, introducing new
Padres uniform. *Photo by Skip Rozin*

Hilly Abzug's birthday party at
Wrigley Field was a bittersweet affair.
Photo by Nancy Abzug

Sharing first base with Pete Rose in Philadelphia, 1980. *Photo by Bob Bartosz*

When we won the pennant in 1981, I thought of Hilly. *AP/Wide World Photos*

Exaltation! Steve Yeager, Steve Howe and I on mound after clinching World Series against Yankees. *AP/Wide World Photos*

Victory parade in Los Angeles with Ron Cey and team. *Los Angeles Times Photo*

"Garvey" on the back of a non-
Dodger uniform was worth a news
conference. *AP/Wide World Photos*

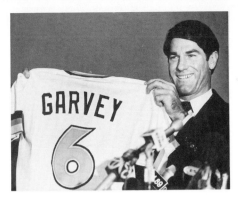

Springtime in Yuma, Arizona . . .
and I was happy to be there. *Photo
by Union-Tribune Publishing Co.*

My first at bat as "the opposition" at
Dodger Stadium tied league
consecutive game streak; fans
showed they hadn't forgotten. *Los
Angeles Times Photo*

Pre-game welcome for ex-teammate Jerry Reuss. *Los Angeles Times Photo*

Billy Williams was there to see me break his record . . . and offer congratulations.
Los Angeles Daily News Photo by Herb Carleton

Three months later, back in San Diego, it ended on this play. *UPI/Bettmann Newsphotos*

For the want of a sound thumb, my streak was lost. *Photo courtesy John Boggs*

Fifth-inning single tied crucial
fourth playoff game against
Cubs. *AP/Wide World Photos*

Four innings later, after
game-winning home run,
pandemonium. *AP/Wide
World Photos*

aping a public service nnouncement during oring training in uma. *Photo by Skip ozin*

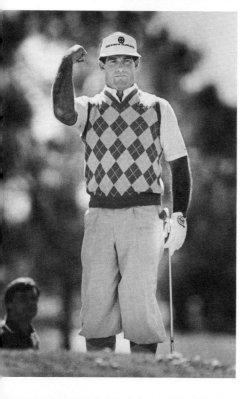

Style on the links. *Photo by Stan Honda*

Tricks for Bankers Systems in St. Cloud, Minnesota. *Photo by Skip Rozin*

Somehow, in the end it always gets back to baseball and kids. *Photo by Skip Rozin*

He got Munson on a line drive to Smith in short right, which brought up Reggie Jackson. Reggie had hit over .400 with two home runs in the playoffs against Kansas City, and hit another in the opener against us. In 1977, of course, he had five.

It was *the* confrontation of the Series. Welch went to 1 and 1, then fed him three fastballs that Jackson could only foul off. A ball, a foul to the screen, and another ball made the count 3–2.

Then, with nearly sixty thousand people standing and screaming, Welch threw a hard fastball up and in. Jackson swung and missed, screwing himself into the batter's box.

It's funny, how some things stick in your mind and some things don't. I can still see Jackson, his body twisted around at the plate; I see him stomping back into the dugout. Everything after that is hazy.

I know we dropped the next four games. I know Graig Nettles made some fantastic plays. I know there was a ten-inning game in which we were ahead; I can see Jackson sticking his hip out to deflect the ball, breaking up a double play, and our losing.

Everything else is a fog. We had won those first two games, turned around and flown to New York, and suddenly everything was different. If there are such things as biorhythms, ours took a collective nose dive.

I do remember, somewhere toward the end—maybe in the last game, after the flight back to Los Angeles; more likely late during the third game at Yankee Stadium, where they blew us out, 12–2—thinking what a frustrating experience this was. I looked out at those big lights, and I thought about Fran Tarkenton with the Minnesota Vikings; all those trips to the Super Bowl, and never a winner. Was I going to go to the World Series all my life and never come away with the big win? I was getting a pretty good start.

GARVEY

As much as anyone, I was to blame. In the six games, I hit .208. No home runs; no RBIs. Everytime I got decent wood on the ball, there was Nettles. My .389 in the playoffs had earned me MVP honors, but believe me it made little difference.

13

During the winter of 1978 I turned thirty, arriving at that milestone with an unexpected legacy of maturity. Sober maturity.

My trouble with some of my Dodger teammates confronted me with the unpleasant reality that being on the same team was not necessarily a strong enough bond for friendship. I had thought otherwise. As a boy, making friends was one of the most appealing things about playing sports. I assumed that situation would continue as a professional. It didn't.

The friction on our team—and especially the fight with Sutton—got a lot of press, and I felt a morbid need to read it all. Seeing comments suggesting that while Sutton was the one taking the swing at me, others would have liked to be in his place, was hurtful. Reading the quotes of players who talked of my passion to be liked as if it were some kind of horrendous affliction only confused me more.

But finally I came to understand. They were saying, "Grow up, Garv. This isn't the playground anymore. Quit talking about love and friendship and hit the ball."

For that time—and for those players—I tried to do just that. It actually became a motivating factor, not to let them affect my play. It may even have stimulated me to be a better ballplayer. Not altogether happier, but better. And more successful.

And I learned of another area where the adult world differed from childhood: Winning.

In Little League and high school, and sometimes even in college, a few really good players could make almost any team a winner. That gives you an incredible feeling of power, and of satisfaction. In the major leagues, it just doesn't work that way. Some people think it does. Some still think, if they're really good enough—hit and run and throw, do all those things they've always done in the past—they can still make a difference. Well, they can make a difference, but in the big leagues they may not be able to make *enough* difference.

That's hard to get used to, and it's one of the big lessons in team sports. No matter how well you play, it may not be enough. One must find a place for that reality.

With all this knowledge in my pocket, I began my thirty-first year in life and my tenth as a Dodger with a great sense of wisdom. Of course my education was just beginning.

The 1979 season was not a memorable one in Dodger history. In fact, when all 162 games were played, it proved to be the least successful I had ever been through.

The problems began long before opening day. Over the winter the club had lost Lee Lacy, Billy North, and, most importantly, Tommy John to free agency. Letting Tommy go, in my view, was a foolish error. Along with Sutton, he had been the backbone of our pitching staff.

Not even I could have guessed how much we would miss Tommy. Terry Forster had elbow surgery during the off season, and never made it back until 1982. Then during the summer, Doug Rau—a dependable starter since 1973—developed shoulder trouble from which he never fully recovered.

We had a shaky April and May, which, in retrospect, looked golden compared to our June, when we won only seven games and dropped fifteen and a half games off the pace. We came back, but never far enough. It was brutal.

For me individually, at least on paper, it wasn't such a bad season, which is to say that my numbers—batting, RBIs, home runs—were good. That's hard to do in a lost season, because the key to performing well is concentration, and concentration is hard to maintain when you are out of the race early. As a matter of personal pride, you have to set some kind of new goal, something other than the championship. I start making up little games, every day, just to keep involved: I want to do better than the other first baseman, or I want to be the best hitter in the game today.

Sometimes there will be a friend or a relative at the game, and I'll want to impress him. Or I'll have met a little boy or girl during batting practice, or I'll know someone who's ill. Maybe it's a birthday, or somebody special is home watching on television. Mental games. Anything to get my pride going. Even if it's negative—not wanting to look bad in front of forty thousand people and a couple of million more on television.

There are days when you just don't have it. Nobody's there to see you. There's no TV. It's nobody's birthday. And worst, the guy who's pitching is really on, and you never did hit him that well to begin with. Still, you try to do something positive—make a play defensively, hit a fly ball and drive in a run. Even move a guy over. You see guys doing that all the time. In spring training, when the team is split into two squads, they meet back at the complex and compare notes: "How'd you do?" "Oh, I advanced a runner." He could say he went 0 for 4, but he's picking something out he did right.

Once you start separating yourself from the game, you're lost. If you're twenty games back in the last month of the season, or ten runs behind in the last inning, you've got to stay in the game.

Concentration, like anything else, is a habit. Permit yourself to begin breaking that habit, and you might as well look for another profession. It is one of my strengths. For two hours or three hours on a ballfield, I'm in my own world. Nothing distracts me; nothing else gets in.

I'll always remember the play Pete Rose made during the last inning of the last game of the 1980 World Series, catching Frank White's foul pop that bounced out of Bob Boone's mit. That was an example of an aggressiveness and anticipation that good players have. They're never out of a game. I smiled when I saw that.

I'm always there by the catcher on a pop up, waiting for the ball to bounce out. One time one did, and I dove and just barely tipped it away. But I'll get one yet.

There are a lot of things you can do to help yourself in baseball, to keep yourself in the game—one game at a time—and to prolong your career. And as I turned thirty, I began thinking a lot about that. I felt at that point I should pick up my off-season conditioning, and spring training, too, so that I could continue to maintain the pace. Not that I felt I was losing anything at that time; I just wanted to make sure I didn't.

My background for physical training came from football—serious high school football and then the Big Ten. The discipline of setting up a schedule of weight training and physical conditioning, and then following it were exactly what I needed. I knew what the goal was, and how to achieve it.

Prior to 1979, I ran in the off-season, lifted some weights—not a lot—and played golf and tennis. But I was quite busy with speaking engagements and traveling. Once the season got going, I didn't do anything special.

That winter I began incorporating more running into my off-season—about three miles now—more weight work, stretching, and eventually I began working in bicycling. For eye-hand coordination during the winter, I still use golf and tennis.

Usually I'll take about a month off before the serious work starts. I think it's important to heal up a little and then go right into working up to your top shape. That process starts in February, and reaches its peak during spring training, the most strenuous time of the year.

I run in the morning, then get to camp about 8 A.M. By 8:15 or 8:20 I'm in the exercise room. The routine changes somewhat, but in the beginning—before the games start—it's quite hectic: jumping rope for 1,000 to 1,500 revolutions. The stationary bike for twenty minutes, alternating intervals of pacing and sprinting, pacing and sprinting. By 9 o'clock I'm out on the field, doing calisthenics with the rest of the squad, running and following their schedule, hitting and taking infield practice. Afterward, it's back into the exercise room for various weight programs. One day it's arms and upper body, the next it's lower body. I work on my stomach muscles every day.

One of the machines I get the most use of is something called "Jaws," designed for strengthening your wrists and forearms. I use it every day; it even travels with us during the season.

I began at seven and eight, building up my forearms by swinging those Dodger bats. Now I use this machine. It has been a thirty-year process of building up the muscles between the wrist and the elbow, just what a hitter needs to generate bat speed. Greater bat speed means you can wait longer on a pitch, giving you a better view of what you're swinging at.

All of this work gets me in my best physical shape of the year by opening day. Baseball shape is something else. That doesn't reach its optimal point until about June 1.

People think you come to camp to get into shape. Wrong. You come to camp in relatively good shape—at the correct weight, having kept up some kind of maintenance program over the winter. Then you refine that for the five weeks of spring training. Fine tuning, really, or at least the beginning of it.

Baseball shape—playing ball, getting back into the rhythm of covering your position, and especially hitting—that begins the first day of spring training. Spring training gets your body and your mind back into a baseball mode, but that's still preseason. Only during the real season can you fine tune yourself into top baseball shape. Only then are the pitchers throwing with their best stuff, are the other players bringing that intensity to every game. They are clearly two different seasons, and should never be confused. What you do in a preseason game is only practice.

After opening day, most of the time is taken up with baseball and travel, but I still work with the dumbells and leg machines about three times a week. I find I can maintain strength for about three days, but after those seventy-two hours it starts to decline.

Of course a program of stretching is crucial. Every day, 40, 45 minutes total. Before the game, during the game some—30 seconds here, 30 seconds there. You need that to maintain maximum flexibility, and you can't start too early.

I also try and watch my diet. More fish and chicken than beef, but I still believe that having beef once a week—twice a week during the season—is necessary for aggressiveness. I find myself becoming more complacent when I eliminate beef totally. I admit that may be purely psychological, but so is a lot of baseball. When I go too long without beef I just don't feel aggressive; I don't drive the ball as well. But in the off-season, hey, I'm a nice guy.

I also eat a lot of salads and fresh vegetables. Fruit, too. Even the ball clubs are beginning to understand about fruit. There are usually oranges and grapefruits in the clubhouse, especially during spring training. And I believe in complex carbohydrates. Pasta. And pancakes. Every morning I have the same thing for breakfast—pancakes, fruit, a large orange juice and tea, and a large glass of water. I try to drink a lot of water. All of this is more controllable at home, but not always easy on the road. So when I travel I take four or five grams of Vitamin C, and a multiple vitamin every day.

Why such a science of the body? When I turned thirty, I began thinking about where I had been and where I was going. We all tend to do that when we reach one of those plateaus. We sum up our accomplishments, and look ahead, making goals for the future. This is where I am, and this is where I want to be in five years, in ten years. As an athlete, I realized I had been pretty much given a free ride as far as my body was concerned. But if I wanted to keep myself on what had been a very satisfying road, I was going to have to start paying a toll.

At nineteen and twenty, there is almost nothing that an athlete can do to his body that is not repairable. His love of the game and the time he puts in just perfecting his skills—his response to the same enthusiasm that kept him playing past dark as a kid—will keep him in shape. He can eat all the junk food he wants. He can sleep four hours a night. I've known rookies who could stay out drinking till dawn, then go out that day and get four hits.

But at thirty—even as early as twenty-five—it begins to affect his body in ways that cannot be so easily fixed. If he doesn't watch what he eats, get involved in a comprehensive program of aerobics, anaerobics, stretching, weight training and eye-hand coordination activities, he's going to lose it all. And he has to do it all year long, to one degree or another. He cannot quit for a month or two, let his body go to pot, then make it back to where he was. You can at twenty, but not at thirty. It just takes too long. At thirty-five it takes even longer. It's the same with excessive eating, with smoking, drinking, and, especially, drugs. All these things are physical and mental detractors.

Very few of the 650 baseball players in the majors took up the game late in life, like at fifteen or sixteen. Most began at six, or maybe seven, the way I did. For most, it's all they know. And as shortsighted as it is, most do not see themselves doing anything else. While no one can play forever, it makes sense to prolong that playing time as much as possible. That is what I am talking about.

Then there's the matter of money.

When I signed a six-year contract with Los Angeles for two million dollars at the beginning of 1977, that looked like a lot of money. It was, and I think everyone involved with the negotiations thought it was fair. I was a twenty-eight-year-old ballplayer who had a career batting average over .300 for his six seasons, with an assortment of Gold Glove and All-Star honors. I was near the top of my game and heading into my most productive years.

Between then and opening day, 1979, some interesting contracts were signed. Larry Hisle, with a career batting average of .272, signed a six-year package reportedly worth $3.16 million; Mike Torrez, with only one twenty-win season in his career, signed a seven-year pact for $2.5 million; Oscar Gamble, a lifetime .264 hitter, signed for $2.85 million over six years.

Free agency may have begun in 1976 with Dave McNally and Andy Messersmith, but the full meaning did not become clear for another three years. Everybody expected the top stars to be signing multi-million-dollar contracts. I don't think anyone envisioned that to filter down to the mid-range players as quickly as it did.

The point I'm making is that nearly every good, steady ballplayer can end up making big money if he stays healthy and puts up some decent numbers. He's not going to make it when he's twenty and still under obligation to the team that brought him along. When he's twenty-seven or thirty—that's when he's going to collect. And if he can stick around till he's thirty-five, all the better.

My situation on the Dodgers was easing considerably by the 1980 season. Most of the antagonists were still around, but some new faces had joined our little drama. Comic faces. Jerry Reuss in 1979; Jay Johnstone in 1980. Reuss was the strong, left-handed pitcher the Dodgers needed after losing Tommy John, and Johnstone was the utility player and pinch hitter we needed since losing Lee Lacy.

They appear from the outside to be quite different: Reuss is six-five and blond, born in Missouri but with a Southern California spirit; Jay is a little shorter, though over six feet, from Connecticut. Jerry is quiet and introspective; Jay, animated and flippant. Jerry throws left and bats right; Jay throws right and bats left.

But they are both quite mad, pranksters to the extreme, and they seemed to recognize me as the perfect straight man. They made fun of everything from my plastic hair to my Popeye forearms to my size. (I'm probably only three inches shorter than Jay, but a full eight inches shorter than Reuss.)

But for all their hijinks, they were appreciated by tiny audiences in the cities where they played, in Houston and Pittsburgh, and in Philadelphia. Los Angeles is the big time for clowns, and they quickly learned that the fastest way to get attention was to hang around me. Every time a photographer appeared to take my picture, there were Reuss and Johnstone, standing beside me. Suddenly they were in the newspapers and on television, their pictures in *Sports Illustrated*.

In return, I got grief.

One night in Atlanta, Reuss put a well-broken-in chaw of tobacco inside the top of my batting helmet. I put it on just before hitting, and this gooey, wet mass began dripping all over my face, all over my uniform.

Another night—we were in San Francisco—somebody stuck a brownie in my glove. I got to first base at the bottom of the inning and put my hand inside, and there was this brown thing. I thought it was a big bug. I ripped off the glove and threw it on the ground. The brownie came out, all melted. I kicked it off the field, but the chocolate had oozed into my glove, around and into the pocket where I catch the ball. By then the inning's going, and I barely get the glove on when the first ball comes to me. I catch it, and now the ball's got chocolate on it. I've got to throw the ball back, so now there's chocolate everywhere.

Back on the bench after the inning, they both stonewalled. "What brownie? Where?" But Johnstone gave it away because there was a little bit of brown crumb on his uniform. I grabbed his hand and smelled his fingers—*chocolate*.

One could become indignant at such episodes; any bank president or university professor surely would. But ballplayers are notorious for their pranks, and I had been too long left out.

John William Johnstone, Jr., twenty-three years a professional baseball player, most recently as a pinch hitter and utility player; returned in 1985 for his second tour with the Dodgers:

"When I first got to the Dodgers in 1980, it was a team with a deep undercurrent of tension. There were no open hostilities—I arrived late for that—but you could feel the tension.

"Tommy Lasorda came to me and said 'Jay, I want you to make my clubhouse fun again. I've heard about you, the kinds of things you've done. Do whatever you have to to get the laughter back.'

"I'd just spent most of two seasons with the Yankees, and I had seen the situation there with Reggie Jackson. But that was somewhat

different. Jackson brought a lot of problems on himself by things he said to the press. Steve brought on his problems just by who he was. That had isolated him.

"But he wasn't the only one in need of special attention. Dave Goltz, who was a very mild-mannered pitcher. Steve Howe. And Reggie Smith, too. We didn't single out Garv—we just had more fun with him.

"I say 'we.' It was me and Jerry Reuss in a mutual nonaggression pact. We would never pull anything on one another, and anybody who tried anything on one got the wrath of both. The plan was to pick on one guy, and set it up so another player would take the blame. That's the team concept.

"Like cutting the crotch out of Rick Sutcliffe's dress shorts, then putting the scissors in Don Stanhouse's locker. Sutcliffe had the shorts on before he realized—the look on his face that second was priceless. He found the scissors. Then he put Stanhouse's sanitaries [baseball socks] and underwear in a pile in the center of the clubhouse, poured lighter fluid on it and set it afire.

"Sometimes we were less devious. Once before a game, Reuss, Stanhouse, and I caught Steve in the outfield and tried to depants him. He got Jerry and me in headlocks, and Don in a scissors grip and wouldn't let go. That sucker's strong.

"Though it began at the suggestion of Lasorda, Steve and I hit it off personally, partly because we have such completely different personalities. He's goody two-shoes; I'm crazy. He could never be like me, but inside he really wants to be. And I had none of the problems with him that some of the other guys did. I wasn't envious of his accomplishments; I admired what he'd done.

"One thing did bother me. He always likes to go out after a game, instead of hanging around the clubhouse. And anyplace we'd go, he gets noticed. And we end up giving out autographs all night. I told him I wasn't going out anymore unless he wore a mask. The most I could ever get him to promise was to wear a hat."

The Dodgers began the 1980 season on the road and losing, but once back home we put together a ten-game winning streak that put us back into the thick of the race, where we stayed throughout the season. By the All-Star break we were about a game behind Houston, not a bad place to be.

Not only was that year's game played in Dodger Stadium, it came in the midst of a two-week home stand, so we didn't even have to travel very far. That was my seventh time playing, and I felt no loss of excitement.

I don't think any of the other all-star games compare with baseball's. First, it's got so much history to it. People still talk about Carl Hubbell striking out Ruth, Gehrig, Foxx, Simmons and Cronin in the 1934 classic.

But even taking each game as it comes, it is an event like no other. It's right in the middle of the summer, so it's got great weather. The fans pick the starting lineups, which gives it the extra element of participation. No other sport has that. And the fact that the players wear their own uniforms gives the game team as well as individual identification.

As I sat in the locker room that afternoon, I thought about some of the great players I had seen play in the game from year to year. Yastrzemski and Frank Robinson, Bobby Bonds and Joe Morgan, Mike Schmidt and Henry Aaron and Pete Rose. I remember thinking about the world's standards of what makes a great player, and my own. For me, it comes down to achievements consistently registered over a long period of time—that viewed against the team's success.

Obviously, Pete Rose fits that niche as well as anybody. He may be the greatest player of our time, the one who, more than any other, has caused his team to win.

I've faced some great pitchers, men who could totally lock up a game. Bob Gibson. Tom Seaver. Juan Marichal. For me, personally, Phil Niekro. James Rodney Richard and Nolan Ryan, both very tough. But still, great as a pitcher is, he only has to go out there and do it once every four or five days. They are different from every-day ballplayers. They are even separated in the Baseball Encyclopedia—Players, and Pitchers.

Every time Rose takes the field, there is a better than even chance that he's going to do something to beat you. If he doesn't get a hit, he's going to walk or advance a runner or do something to cause a run to score. And if he doesn't do it at the plate, he'll do it from the field. It may not always be pretty, but the job will get done. One way or another, he affects the game in his team's favor. And he's usually there to do it. The greatest talent in the world does his team no good on the disabled list. Year in and year out, Rose has proven to be a remarkably durable athlete; in ten different seasons he's played in every game.

Bench was a player who was always in the game, and, for a catcher, unusually durable. Thurman Munson was another one; Lou Brock another. These guys were always there, and always looking for a way to beat you. I'm not ignoring players like Rod Carew and Bill Madlock. They're both great hitters for average; Carew will surely end up in the Hall of Fame. But Rose—like them, a contact hitter—has scored so many more runs: over one hundred in ten different seasons.

I happened to be looking at Carew's stats recently. No run production. Very rarely has he scored one hundred runs, and rarely had he driven in one hundred—once, actually, the year he hit .388. He played on some pretty good offensive teams in Minnesota, and since he's moved to the Angels. He has always gotten his hits. But when all is said and done, the name of the game is still run production. That's how you win.

Madlock is a similar case. A great hitter for average. Four batting titles. But never one hundred runs scored or driven in. Part of the reason is that he's often out of the lineup with injuries, which limits what he can do to win ball games.

For the Dodgers to win games that 1980 season, we needed help from a lot of people. We were plagued by injuries; the lineup changed constantly. Reggie went down with a shoulder injury toward the end of July, which was about the time Cey got hot. Russell smashed a finger early in September, and Derrel Thomas took over for him.

We were even with Houston with ten days left. Then they won six of their next seven and we dropped four of seven, again, mostly on the road. That gave them a three-game lead with three to play. But those three were at Dodger Stadium.

That first game was on Friday night; only two guys from the starting eight on opening day were in the lineup—Dusty and me, and Dusty was hurting. There was an excitement in the air. The crowd was much noisier than normal before a game. The national anthem had just been played, and you could feel the fans starting to get each other up, starting to clap.

I stood at the corner of the dugout by the steps with a towel around my shoulders, just watching. Then for some reason—on impulse—I started twirling the towel in the air. The fans saw me, and they began to respond. The noise got louder and louder and louder. We took the field to a thunderous ovation.

That really energized the guys. The previous couple of days the papers had written about this team having guts, how they had kept coming back from injuries, never giving up, and how it was all coming down to these three games.

We went into the ninth inning trailing 2–1. We tied it with two outs on Ron Cey's single. In the tenth, Joe Ferguson won the game on a home run. We were all waiting for him at home plate, the whole team, jumping all over one another. Everybody went wild. The players, the fans. Everybody.

Dodger Stadium fans are very knowledgeable, and they're relatively courteous to the other team. They know when to applaud, and they don't usually lose their composure. So this was unusual. It was as if they said, "This team is down and it's hurt and we're going to pick 'em up. We're going to take it into our own hands."

The next day before the game I was standing in the dugout with Fred Claire, vice president in charge of public relations, and discussing how fabulous the fans were. Neither of us has ever seen Dodger fans behave like that. I said it was as if they were our "tenth player." Fred liked that; the next day, papers were full of references to "the tenth player."

This time the fans were standing and applauding before we ever took the field. They seemed to know they could have an effect. Reuss pitched a 2–1 victory over Nolan Ryan; I drove in both runs, one with a home run. Now we trailed by one.

On Sunday afternoon we had the biggest crowd of the season, over 52,000 people. This was the last game on the schedule.

We fell behind 3–0 after four innings. Then we started coming back. We scored one run in the fifth on three singles, and another in the seventh on Mota's pinch hit, though we left the bases loaded. In the eighth I reached on an error, and Cey—who was hobbled by a hamstring injury—fouled off a dozen pitches, one off of his own foot. Finally he drove one over the 385-foot marker and into the left field pavilion.

Leading 4–3, Steve Howe got into trouble in the ninth. And with two on and two out, Sutton came in to get the final out. We had tied Houston on the final day of the regular season.

From the sixth inning on, the fans were on their feet and cheering. They brought Cey and Sutton out of the dugout over and over, refusing to let the moment die.

Unfortunately, it did die. The next day in the special one-game playoff, Joe Niekro shut us down, 7–1.

It was the single greatest series I had ever been involved in. For fans, for players, for everybody. And, for a season in which we did ultimately lose, it was not only memorable but also inspirational.

14

It was in 1980 that I was contacted by *Inside Sports,* the magazine that had been started by *Newsweek* to compete with *Sports Illustrated.* A freelance writer named Pat Jordan wanted to interview me for an "in-depth story." Jordan had spent a brief time as a pitcher in the Braves organization and later wrote intelligently about the experience. I didn't give it any special thought; by then there had been many reporters and many articles. I said okay.

But when he arrived, he spent only a small amount of time with me, and considerably more interviewing Cyndy. It was a difficult time for Cyndy. The girls were now four and six years old, and she had been working in television in Los Angeles for about two years and doing very well.

That in itself caused some problems, though it was no different from the situation a lot of couples find themselves in today. Two people and two careers. I had my responsibilities as an athlete. She had her responsibilities as a television interviewer and co-host. And we had our responsibilities as partners in a marriage and as parents. Those conflicts had begun to pull us away from one another. And there were other problems, caused by baseball and the complex little world in which it exists.

Cyndy enjoyed the game. Growing up with two brothers who played baseball, and being married to me, she learned the game well. But even when we were first married and she'd make 85 to 90 percent of the home games, her interest was mainly in me. She'd watch the game, but she'd also bring a book. When I wasn't hitting, she would read.

After Krisha was born, Cyndy went to fewer games. And when Whitney came along—in the summer of 1976—that number continued to drop. Once she started working, attending became even harder. She still made some games during the week, but mostly she came to home games on weekends. And whenever she did attend—in the early years alone, or later on with the girls—she drew a lot of attention. People had seen her on television, or in magazines and newspapers, and they recognized her. And the other players' children were naturally drawn to her; she is pretty, and very warm.

All of this helped separate her from the other wives. It was not so different from my own situation with many of the Dodgers. But while the players and I weren't close off the field, playing together gave the appearance of great friendship. The wives had only their off-the-field activities—socializing in the stands, or away from the park—and Cyndy was rarely a part of those.

Feathers were ruffled because of that, and I'm sorry. But she wasn't under contract to the Dodgers. Only I was. Still, she got dragged into everything. When the stories of my estrangement from some of my teammates implicated her, she took a lot of flack. As I said earlier, the argument with Don Sutton came to blows because he threw Cyndy into the mix.

It all put terrible pressure on her, especially when added to a series of horrendous incidents that included harrassment and even death threats. Some came anonymously, made against me through the club, or were telephoned to the hotel where I stayed on the road. Some of the harrassment was more direct.

One night, after a game at Dodger Stadium, a woman was waiting for me by my car. She was about twenty-five, wearing slacks, a blue windbreaker, and tennis shoes. She asked for an autograph, and I gave it to her. She said she wanted to talk. I told her I was late. She insisted; I apologized.

She was there the next night, and the next, and the next. She would stand in the way so I couldn't close the car door. The following night I had two plainclothes policemen go out with me, and she got violent. She scratched one of the policemen's face, drawing blood, and then turned on the other.

One day game later that season, Cyndy brought the girls. The woman saw them and almost knocked Krisha down the escalator. After the All-Star luncheon at the Biltmore Hotel in 1980, she was waiting by a side entrance, and when she saw us coming out, she elbowed Cyndy in the ribs, bruising her badly.

It got to the point where Cyndy couldn't show up at a game without being harrassed by her—pushed and assaulted and threatened. I finally had to take out a restraining order, just so my wife would attend a game. Even after that, my mother-in-law saw her one morning walking on the street outside our house. She called the police, but the woman ran away.

These bizarre incidents added to the tensions that came along naturally with our own lives. I was in the midst of the consecutive game streak in 1980, and intensely involved with being the best ballplayer I could be. Cyndy, in addition to being a wife and mother, was making a name for herself in her own career, as Cyndy Garvey and not just Mrs. Steve Garvey.

At the same time she was living in another world, and there she was the wife of a professional baseball player and put under enormous pressure because of that. The pressure got in the way of everything she was trying to accomplish, and she felt great anxiety because of it.

That was the scene into which Pat Jordan stumbled. It never occurred to me that it would end up in the story; I thought the focus of the piece was baseball. When it came out, in the August issue of *Inside Sports*, I discovered baseball was not the subject.

The article, about nine thousand words long, was broken into seven sections of varying lengths, each bearing a short, almost accusatory headline: "THE WIFE," "THE JOB" (her job, not mine), "THE PROBLEM."

It all came under the title TROUBLE IN PARADISE.

Selected quotes from the *Inside Sports* article, along with the names of their respective sections:

THE HOUSE

All the photographs were the same. Stylized. Posed. Perfect exposures without a blemish. . . .

All the mementos were the same. Unblemished. Disposable. There were no cheap objects purchased when the husband was struggling; no slightly more expensive objects purchased as the husband's fortunes improved slowly. There was no unused space. It was as if, for this family, all these expensive-looking objects were needed to fill in the gaps in their unformed natures.

THE WIFE

Cyndy Garvey is 30 years old. She is tall and thin. She has long blond hair. She is pretty in the manner of a Miss America contestant, a look she embellishes—bleached hair, heavy makeup—to give it distinction. It is a look thought glamorous in certain regions of this country, and despite her protestations ("I don't try to look this way. I just always was glamorous"), it is not a look acquired without effort. She claims her looks are a burden, which is not uncommon among women who have been pretty all their lives.

THE HUSBAND

Garvey hops up the dugout steps and breaks into a trot toward first base while his teammates are taking pregame batting practice. He moves precisely, almost in slow motion. He is conscious of the way he runs and of the fact that he is being watched. His pumping arms are properly bent into Ls at his sides, and held away from his body a bit, like wings, as if to keep his shirt from wrinkling. He resembles a man trotting to catch a bus in a new silk shirt on a hot day.

A fan in the stands calls out his name. Without breaking stride, Garvey glances back over his shoulder and smiles. It is an odd smile, both humble and smug. It is automatic, like someone who is used to smiling in public, even when the occasion does not demand it, just as a foreigner smiles too readily at things he does not understand.

There was much more, and very little of it pleasant. In describing me, in the midst of an interview with a sportswriter: "He looks down and flutters his eyelids as he speaks. It is meant to be a humbling gesture." Describing Cyndy in a restaurant: "It is the smile of a woman who thinks she is being sexy. It is merely a dessert filled with empty calories."

I read the piece over several times, and it was hard to know what angered me more—the quotes of Cyndy's words of frustration taken out of context, or the snide remarks. The agonizing thing is there was a real story he happened across, a story of people in transition, of a two-career family where both parties are highly visible, the pressure that creates; and mostly, the story of a woman finding her way in a world of shifting values.

Had he reported that story straight—let the people and the situation speak for themselves—he would have had something that said something important about our times. I might still have been upset to see it in print, but I couldn't have cried foul, and I would have had no legal recourse. But he didn't. By his nasty, condescending references to who we were and how we lived, his prejudice as a reporter distorted whatever merit the piece might have had.

I discussed the matter with Cyndy. Then we had a meeting with Alan Rothenberg, our lawyer. We talked about the legalities of the situation—what is malice, what is defamation. Then we discussed the chances of winning a lawsuit against *Inside Sports* and *Newsweek*. We decided to sue for libel.

In retrospect, it was probably a mistake. We ended up settling out of court. And while we pretty much broke even on expenses and legal fees, the enormous amount of aggravation is something you can't put a price on. The time, the anxiety, the strain, the trips to New York for taking depositions.

But we were so angry. We felt the whole thing had been so shabby, so immoral, that to accept it would be to compound the sin. What I wanted to do was to take the magazine by its corporate lapels and shake it. It wasn't just Pat Jordan. You don't have that kind of article, that length, laid out that way, with juicy lines blown up as teasers, without an editorial decision saying, "Good, let's get 'em." What we probably should have done was to call a press conference, declare that the article was a collection of half-truths and quotes taken out of context, and walk away.

But it was getting more complicated by the minute. After the article appeared, the *Los Angeles Herald-Examiner* planned to publish a five-part series excerpted from it. *Inside Sports* and the *Herald-Examiner* are both owned by the Hearst Corporation.

We took out an injunction to stop them, at least till the libel suit was settled. The court issued a temporary restraining order, but in the meantime the *Los Angeles Times* printed pieces of the story, so we were surrounded by it.

Whatever strains existed between Cyndy and me because of the circus accompanying my life were magnified by the *Inside Sports* drama and the mass of publicity that it generated. Cyndy's difficulties with that circus were made the focus, so she received the bulk of the criticism. It was all very unfair, and it helped drive us apart.

The experience taught me something about the press that I had been slowly learning but did not want to confront. There are people in the business who enjoy discovering something and then building it up, and enjoy all the more tearing it down, destroying it in public.

Cyndy and I never introduced ourselves as the All-American couple. The press did. It's true that I enjoyed that image. I thought it was healthy and positive. And I did my best to live up to it. But I never said there were no flaws.

When flaws appeared in our marriage, the press jumped all over us as if it were a personal offense to them, and began stomping on the image they had created.

It's all part of being a public figure, another lesson I was slow in learning. Though it would take me several more years to come to the decision, I finally concluded that the personal aspects of my life—such as with whom I am sharing my most private moments—are better left out of the news. I think my candor cost me in the past. I regret that I must be less open today.

15

Even during spring training of 1981, there was a looseness to the club, which translated to confidence on the field. It was as if that final drive at the end of the 1980 season was carrying over emotionally to the new season. Though we lost the final game, we were a team that knew we could win under pressure.

There were some significant changes in the opening day lineup. Ken Landreaux, who had come over from Minnesota during the winter, was in center field. And we had two young players from our own system: Pedro Guerrero in right field and Mike Scioscia behind the plate.

But the new name that had the greatest impact was Fernando Valenzuela. Seeing him in the locker room, walking around with his shirttail hanging out, you might not have guessed. He was not an imposing figure—five-ten, around 200 pounds, with a pudgy face. Purchased from the Mexican League in 1979, he spoke not a word of English when he was called up to the Dodgers late the following summer. They said he was twenty. He looked more like a thirty-six-year-old who had abused his younger years.

But he could pitch. He is a left-hander, and he had a screwball that broke down and away from a right-handed batter—just the opposite of a curve. It was close to impossible to hit. It also made his other pitches—he had a good curve, a slider, and a better-than-average fastball—all the more effective.

The Dodgers brought him up midway through September, when we were trying to catch Houston. He worked out of the bullpen and did not give up a single earned run in the ten games in which he relieved.

Jerry Reuss was supposed to open at home in 1981 against Houston, but he had a sore shoulder. Burt Hooton was next in line, but he wasn't quite ready either. Valenzuela ended up with the opening day assignment, and he pitched a five-hit shutout; we won, 2–0. Over the next seven starts he gave up just four earned runs as he ran his personal record to 8–0 and placed the Dodgers securely in first place.

When you look back at the 1981 season, it falls naturally into two halves, with the baseball strike coming in the middle. Clearly, the first half belonged to Fernando. He was so dominant. Especially during those first two months, he was untouchable. He had the control and poise of a veteran, and ended up leading the league in every positive category—from strikeouts to shut-outs to innings pitched. He is the only man ever to win the Cy Young and Rookie of the Year awards in the same season.

In my memory, there has never been a pitcher who broke in with such a splash. Mark Fidrych, who came up with Detroit in 1976, got a lot of people excited, but that was more his personality than his pitching prowess. Even Dwight Gooden, effective as he was in his first season with the Mets, did not have the same impact.

Fernando was an event. This youngster from northwestern Mexico, the last of twelve children in a poor family, was a genuine phenomenon. He really wasn't fat; more barrel-chested, with a big body. While he spoke no English, he accepted the carnival that sprang up around him with remarkable good nature, always smiling.

And it was a carnival. Everywhere we played, the crowds came to see Number 34, with his unorthodox windup, where he rolls his eyes to the sky, then uncoils with a screwball nobody can hit. And while he was earning the league minimum as a rookie, by season's end he was receiving ten thousand dollars for every outside appearance.

But no place was he more popular than in Los Angeles. Bus loads of fans came from below the border every time he pitched, and thousands of Mexican-Americans came to the park. He was an international star; that first month we even had a television crew from Sweden.

All that hoopla might have gotten to some people—the T-shirts, the records, the books—but not Fernando. He just kept smiling and pitching. And he has continued to develop. His beginning in the 1985 season—giving up no earned runs in his first four starts and only one earned run in his first five—was astonishing.

We've seen, over and over, that continued success does not always follow a great start. With pitchers the problem is often an injury; for example, Fidrych, and also Wayne Simpson. Simpson posted a 13–1 record through the first half of his rookie season with Cincinnati, then developed arm trouble and disappeared.

But sometimes there is no apparent reason, no torn ligament or rotator cuff to blame. I remember when Butch Metzger came up with the Padres in 1976—a good relief pitcher with what looked like a bright future. But the following season he struggled, and San Diego traded him to St. Louis. Within a year he was back in the minors, and then he was gone completely.

There are far more Butch Metzgers than there are Fernandos in baseball. Joe Charboneau was a hero in Cleveland in his first season. And that was it—one season, 1980—and he faded into oblivion. Steve Blass was a nineteen-game winner and World Series star for Pittsburgh in 1972. The next year he couldn't find home plate; within two seasons he was gone.

The skills of this profession are God-given, and they can abandon us without any warning. It happens every day. We all know it, but none of us likes to think about it. So when you see an athlete like Fernando come along, you almost hold your breath. He seems so good, so complete. Not just throwing the ball. He could field; he was even a decent hitter. And the fans loved him. All the fans. Sure, he was something special to the Chicano community. But the Beverly Hills set was just as excited. He even turned them on in spring training.

Those people at Vero Beach are knowledgeable fans. They had seen the way he pitched in the final series against Houston in 1980, and they welcomed him the way they had so many young rookies. They are part of what makes coming to Dodgertown such a memorable experience.

Spring training is really your closest contact with fans. Things are so much more hectic during the season; then you perceive "fans" as tens of thousands of screaming people in the stands. At Vero you get to know people as individuals. I remember a sweet lady, Bess Lockhart, who came down from her home in Columbus, Georgia every spring. I remember Jess Collyer, who for ten years had been mayor of Ossining, New York. These people were there every year. Some were residents of Vero Beach; others came south from New York and Chicago, timing their vacations with the opening of camp.

To some you only said hello. Others you got to know a little better. In some cases, they even touched your life. That was the case with Nancy and Hilly Abzug. Hilly was an internist in Chicago, but he was born in Brooklyn, and was a life-long Dodger fan. I first noticed him at Dodgertown during the spring of 1975. He was easy to spot, and not because he was six feet tall, over 200 pounds, and bearded. He was the only man there wearing a T-shirt that said Brooklyn Dodgers. He told me he had attended his first Dodger came at Ebbets Field when he was eight. Brooklyn beat Milwaukee that day, 12–8. In 1957, when the Dodgers left Brooklyn, so did Hilly. The team went to Los Angeles; he went to Chicago to study medicine. But his heart remained in Flatbush.

I ended up seeing Hilly and Nancy a lot in the years that followed. They attended every game in Chicago, and were in Vero Beach every spring. And somewhere along the road, in Cincinnati or St. Louis, in Pittsburgh or Montreal or even Houston, there they'd be, rooting for the Dodgers. Always waving, always in their Brooklyn Dodger T-shirts that Hilly had had specially made. Originally he had them in several colors, but Lasorda convinced him if it's a Dodger shirt it's got to be blue and white, so he burned the other colors. They were fans.

Then in 1979 Hilly got sick. Cancer of the colon. I saw him in 1979, and in 1980, too. He was so big, so robust. He didn't look sick. And he didn't act sick.

Hilly died in 1981, while the players were out on strike. In October, when we defeated the Yankees in the World Series, our clubhouse was bedlam, jammed with television crews, photographers, and reporters. I was celebrating, just like the rest of my teammates. I had my uniform shirt off; underneath was one of Hilly's Brooklyn Dodger shirts.

When the press asked me about it I just told them it was for a friend . . . and a great Dodger fan.

Mrs. Nancy Abzug, widow of Dr. Hillyard Abzug:

"It was really a very superficial relationship. But in a way it wasn't. They were never going to be best friends, but there was a warmth and sincerity between the two of them that didn't just come from my husband dying.

"Before then there had been the casual encounters: We had break-fast once with Steve in Montreal. Then at spring training, we hap-pened to be at a restaurant where Cyndy and the girls were; we sat with them.

"I was planning a special surprise for Hilly's 45th birthday, but in 1980 that was still a year away and I wasn't sure he would make it. So I decided to celebrate his 44th. I bought fifty tickets to Wrigley Field when the Dodgers were coming in, and had fifty shirts made up that said BROOKLYN DODGERS *on the front, and* HILLY'S 44TH BIRTHDAY *on the back. I talked to Steve, and he was able to get Hilly on the field that day. Hilly was ecstatic. It was a Wednesday, July 16. I've still got the photograph of them together on the field.*

"A year later my husband was dying. We knew it was going to happen so I brought him home from the hospital. Somebody must have told Steve, because the Friday before Hilly died he called.

"I picked up the phone and he said 'Hi, Nance, it's Steve. I hear Hilly's pretty sick. Can I talk to him?'

"Hilly had been in a semi-coma, and hadn't talked for about ten or twelve hours. There were several friends in the house, and we had taken turns talking to him all day, but there had been no response. He just lay there. I'd heard that sometimes if you really shake somebody in that state he can hear. So I shook him hard, and I said it was Steve Garvey on the phone. Just like that, he snapped out of it.

"They talked for a few minutes. Hilly said hi and asked him about the players' strike, when did he think it was going to be over. Then he asked him how he was doing, and about the girls. It was the most normal-sounding conversation. After about eight, nine sentences, he stopped, and fell back into the coma. He never spoke another word to anyone. On Sunday morning at 10 o'clock Hilly died."

The Reds came on to challenge early in June, and we barely held on to a half-game lead as negotiations between the owners and the players union broke down. The strike was called for Friday morning, June 12.

I actually owe my consecutive game streak to that strike. About a week before I had sprained my wrist while trying to check my swing, and it was becoming increasingly more difficult to swing the bat. It was my right hand, the top hand when I bat. The top hand generates my power, and the bottom hand is the guide hand. I could make contact, but I couldn't drive the ball with any power.

During that last game in St. Louis, I told Lasorda that he had better send Reggie Smith in to hit for me. It was late in the game and we were down a run. That was one of the few times I was ever pinch hit for as a Dodger, and the only time I ever took myself out of a game. If there had been no strike, I'd have had to sit out to let the wrist heal. The consecutive game streak would have ended. At that point I was up to 892 games, just 225 behind Billy Williams' National League record.

But there was a strike, because the owners and the players couldn't agree on compensation for free agents. And instead of flying to Pittsburgh to face the Pirates in a weekend series, we flew home to Los Angeles for my first summer vacation in many years.

In the eight weeks that we were off, the wrist healed completely. I also got a chance to spend some extra time with my daughters. We went to Hawaii; we went to Disneyland—all the things I had never been able to do with them in the summer. At the same time, I did my best to stay in shape.

Because of the commissioner's formula for dealing with that season, our leading the west at the point the strike began made us, in effect, the winner of the First Half. Those post-strike games constituted the Second Half, which began afresh for everyone on August 10. The leader at season's end then played the First Half winner in a mini-playoff.

That plan meant that we were in the mini-playoff no matter how well—or poorly—we played during August and September, which took some incentive out of those final fifty-three games. The big loser was Cincinnati, who ended up with the best record in the league—in all baseball, actually—but won neither the First Half nor the Second Half and so got no closer to the playoffs or the World Series than their television sets.

Houston won the Second Half by one and a half games over the Reds. We hung close through most of the summer, then faded the last two weeks, not that it mattered.

The five-game playoff opened in the Astrodome with a classic match-up between Valenzuela and Nolan Ryan. The score was 1–1 through eight innings. Fernando was lifted for a pinch hitter in the top of the ninth, and in the bottom of the inning Alan Ashby hit a two-run homer off Dave Stewart for a 3–1 victory.

The second game matched Jerry Reuss against Joe Niekro, and went scoreless through ten innings. Dennis Walling singled home Phil Garner in the eleventh for the only run of the game.

Suddenly we were back in Los Angeles, one game away from ending the season. Sound familiar?

Before the first game at Dodger Stadium, while we were taking batting practice, the Astros were very casual. Some were sitting on the railing; some were even in the stands. Many were just standing around talking, confident to the point of being nonchalant. We scored three times in the first inning—two more than we'd managed in twenty innings in Houston—and Burt Hooton gave us seven innings of three-hit pitching. We won, 6–1, and trailed two games to one.

The next day was Saturday, and before the game Houston looked a little more attentive. But not much. There was a little ball tossing, but there were also a lot of guys leaning on the railing, talking. They still felt that was going to be their afternoon. You could read it in their faces. The stadium was packed, just as it was that last weekend of the 1980 season. Fernando gave up only four hits and held them scoreless till the ninth, and we won, 2–1.

Now we're even, two wins apiece. You should have seen the Astros before the Sunday game: They're playing pepper, they're running in the outfield. Everybody's moving; nobody's standing around. But it was too late. Jerry Reuss pitched a five-hit shutout, and Nolan Ryan gave up three runs in the sixth inning en route to a 4–0 Los Angeles win.

I'll never forget that last out. With two down and nobody on, they sent up Dave Roberts to pinch-hit. Reuss got him to swing at a third strike, but Mike Scioscia, our catcher, missed the ball and it went to the screen. Roberts didn't see it, and started to walk back to the dugout. Scioscia ran after the ball as Roberts, realizing his mistake, took off for first. It was an afternoon game, and by then we were half in shadows, half in sunlight. Mike chased down the ball, and threw to me out of the shadows. Roberts dove for the bag as I lunged for the throw, which was in the dirt. I barely kept my foot on the bag, then fell down as the game ended and everybody ran onto the field.

That series taught me something I'll never forget. It said to me, "Never, never let up! Never take anything for granted!" When you're going well, pour it on and keep that pressure on. Not just in a series, but in a game. If you've scored four runs, go for five. If you, personally, have three hits and it's your last time up, try for four. Never waste an at-bat; never waste an opportunity to score. Take nothing for granted. Never assume a game is won or that you've done enough. That momentum can always stop, or it can switch to the other team. Sports is one of society's accepted outlets for expressing aggressiveness. So do it—be aggressive on the field.

That was how we played the first game of the playoffs against Montreal, aggressively. They had won their series with Philadelphia, three games to two, and were in Los Angeles to start the League Championships. Scioscia and Guerrero hit home runs and Davey Lopes stole two bases as we took a one game lead behind Burt Hooton, 5–1. It felt good.

But then something happened. They beat Fernando in the second game on a five-hit shutout by Ray Burris, and took the first game in Montreal, 4–1, behind Steve Rodgers. Suddenly we were back in the hole. One win in the remaining two games at home and Montreal would go to the World Series.

Playing in the fourth game, the score was tied 1–1 in the eighth inning. Bill Gullickson, a young, hard-throwing right hander was on the mound. It had been cold, and I could tell he had been pitching tight the whole game. I knew what he was thinking. A pitcher who suspects he's losing some velocity late in a game is reluctant to throw fast balls, especially to a power hitter. I told Paul Padilla, our trainer, who was sitting next to me on the bench, that he was going to throw me a slider.

With one out, Dusty Baker singled. Up I came, thinking slider all the way. He threw me a slider over the plate, and I hit it high over the left field fence. That made it 3–1. We scored four more times in the ninth, tying the series at two games apiece.

Playing baseball in Montreal in October is only good if there's a heat wave. There was no heat wave in 1981. It was chilly for the first two games, and just plain miserable for the finale, scheduled for Sunday afternoon. Freezing rain. Finally, after three and a half hours, they postponed it.

Monday wasn't much better—about 45 degrees, and wet. They waited half an hour, then started. Fernando gave up a run in the bottom of the first; Tim Raines scored on a double play. Then he shut them down completely. Meantime, he drove in the tying run himself on a ground out in the fourth. In the ninth inning, Steve Rodgers, their top starter, came in to pitch. He got me and Cey, but Rick Monday sent a 3 and 1 pitch deep and high into center field, and over the fence. Valenzuela ran into trouble in the bottom of the inning, walking Gary Carter and Larry Parrish with two out, but Welch came in to get the final out and end the game and the series.

We were starting to feel charmed. Down 2–0 to Houston, we had come back to win. Down 2–1 to Montreal and on the road, we came back to win. You could start to see a plot forming, even a destiny there. Maybe, after all the adversity, this was going to be *the year*.

Because of the rainout on Monday, we lost our scheduled day off between the playoffs and the start of the World Series. We flew to New York and opened up the following night.

I won't say we were flat in the first two games. They simply executed well and we didn't. Ron Guidry and Rich Gossage pitched well in the first game, and my old buddy Tommy John, again with help from Gossage, shut us out in the second. So there we were again, trailing two games to none. But the guys weren't down. We knew we were heading back to Dodger Stadium, and our fans there give us an advantage. And we would have Valenzuela. He had been tough all year, but especially tough at Dodger Stadium.

That turned out to be one of his guttier performances. He was in a lot of jams, threw a lot of pitches. We were ahead early, fell behind, then came back and won. Fernando gave up seven walks and nine hits, but only four runs. We won, 5–4.

We fell behind the next day, too. It was 4–0 before we scored our first run in the fourth inning, narrowing their lead to 4–2. But then it was 6–3 in the sixth inning when Jay Johnstone came to the plate as a pinch hitter with a man on and blasted a Ron Davis fastball into the right centerfield stands, pulling us within one. Lopes then lifted a fly ball to right that Reggie Jackson let bounce off his chest for a two-base error, and Russell singled to tie the score at 6–6. We pushed two more runs across in the seventh, then hung on while Steve Howe weathered the final innings. It wasn't pretty, but it got us even at two games apiece.

Game Five was on Sunday, and Reuss pitched a beauty, giving up one run on five hits over the nine innings. Guerrero and Yeager hit back to back home runs in the seventh, and that was all we needed for the 2–1 win.

There was one terrifying moment in the eighth inning. With Gossage in for Guidry, one of his fastballs sailed and struck Ron Cey on the left side of the batting helmet. Cey crumpled like he'd been shot. He fell to the ground, holding his head. They rushed him to the hospital for X rays, but he was fine and on the plane to New York with the rest of us. Hard as Gossage throws—that pitch was clocked at 94 miles an hour—there is no question that the helmet saved Ron's life.

We lost a day in New York because of rain; I think everybody welcomed the extra rest.

The sixth game began in a civilized enough fashion. We were tied at one after four innings. Hooton for us; Tommy John for them. Then in the bottom of the fourth, Nettles doubled with one out, and Cerone struck out. We walked Larry Milbourne, their shortstop, to get to John, and the Yankees lifted the pitcher for a pinch hitter, Bobby Murcer. Everybody was shocked—

John had looked so sharp. Murcer's flying out was almost anticlimatic.

George Frazier took over in the fifth inning, and the roof fell in. We scored three in the fifth, and four more in the sixth. The suspense was over. From then on all we had to do was play out the game, and we would be world champions.

During those final innings—while in the dugout waiting to hit, in the field while Steve Howe was warming up—there was time to think. Not consciously—foremost in your mind is always the game. But somewhere in the deep recesses, as my eyes scanned those brilliant lights, my memory flashed back to 1977 and 1978, to Reggie hitting home runs and Lou Piniella getting his hits, to Thurman Munson and that play at the plate when Nestor Chylak called me out. (I've still got a picture of my foot on the plate before the tag.) Jackson's hip deflecting that double play ball in '78, and their winning by one run. My hitting a line drive at Piniella in the first inning of a game, and the two runs that never scored. More line shots and Graig Nettles always at the other end. How many RBIs? Maybe four? How many victories lost?

One after another, flashes of memory. Pearl Bailey singing the national anthem for what seemed like ten minutes. Standing there, wanting to get on with the game, but really enjoying what she was bringing to it. You can see Steinbrenner's box from the field. When they were winning, there seemed to be a glow from there. That night it was dark and silent.

I thought of 1955, which was the first Dodger World Series win, and the team that I met that next spring in Tampa. The Yankees had won the first two games that year, too, and those Dodgers—my first Dodgers—had fought back to win.

In the seventh inning, before my last at bat, I remember thinking of that fifth game in 1978. By my last at bat, the game seemed lost. We were lost. I honestly questioned if we would ever make it all the way. Three times we had made it into the World Series, and three times we had lost. But there we were, back again. And this time, we were winners.

With two outs and a man on in the ninth, Jackson was up against Steve Howe. He kept battling the ball off, foul after foul, and finally hit a hard two-hopper to Lopes. Davey couldn't handle it and Jackson was on. When he reached first, I said to him, "You really didn't want to make the last out, did you?" He shook his head: "You know how it is."

And I knew just what he meant. I never want to make the last out of the game. I don't want the game to end because of me, and that's it. Even ten runs down, I get fanatical about making the last out. The other side of that is that I always want to handle the last chance. I wanted to that night. Bob Watson was up, and I was hoping a ground ball would be hit to someone and they'd throw to first. Two divisional playoffs and the series against Houston had ended that way, with the final balls coming to me. The last play of the Houston and Montreal series, I ended up on my knees. A little theatrical, I guess, but I loved it. But not this time. Watson hit a fly ball to Kenny Landreaux in center.

I broke into an 880-stride toward Steve Howe, getting to the mound just as Yeager did, and there was this great celebration, with everybody jumping up and down. My hat came off and I reached for it. Just then a fan grabbed out and snatched it away from me. I said, "Gimme that hat!" He handed it back; I couldn't believe it. I thought I was going to have to tackle him.

I can still see Lasorda coming out of the dugout in a dead run, his little legs pumping up and down and his portly body not getting anywhere. But he was coming, calling out, "You gotta believe! You gotta believe!" And then there he was in the midst of us, jumping on everybody, hugging me, hugging Howe.

We boarded the Dodger plane late that night. There was still a lot of partying, lots of congratulations. Everybody was quite affectionate, which was great. Winning does that. It dulls the past, and unifies the present. That was our first championship—Los Angeles had won before, but none of us was there—and everybody felt good. No old anger; no old jealousy.

About two hours out of New York it hit them—the excitement, the fatigue, the champagne. Suddenly they were all out. I couldn't sleep. I walked to the back of the plane, stood there looking out over my sleeping teammates. My mind continued along the route begun earlier in the evening, sliding back over the years, from my own backyard in Tampa to the Dodger bus, from Chamberlain High to Ogden to Los Angeles, and from the frustration of 1977 and 1978 to the elation of 1981. I thought about how much I had wanted it all, and what it meant to me now that I had it.

Winning was wonderful—as wonderful as I ever thought it would be. But you never forget the pain. The rejection of your teammates, the pressures on your marriage. That September, Cyndy and the girls had gone to New York. While we would talk later of getting back together, by that time we would both be seeing other people. The marriage was essentially over.

The winning was just what I dreamed it would be. But the price was greater than I had ever imagined.

The plane landed at 6 A.M. You couldn't believe what was waiting for us. Two columns of people, six deep, waiting from our gate all the way out of the building and into the street. Thousands of people, all screaming. Lights. Confetti. People trying to grab you, to touch you. I had four security men around me in a diamond, just so I could get by with my clothes still on.

The next day we had a parade down through the city of Los Angeles, culminating at City Hall. There were awards and presentations and speeches. I remember that next week, going into restaurants and receiving standing ovations. People would stop eating their dinner, stand, and applaud.

Not bad for a kid who started out hitting grapefruit with a broomstick.

16

Two questions were repeated over and over prior to the start of the 1982 season: (1) Could the Dodgers repeat as world champions? (2) Had management contacted me about re-signing?

I had no difficulty with the first. We could win again. We were a solid team with an excellent blend of veteran talent and good-looking players coming up from the farm system. That is the ideal combination. The only regular from '81 not back was Davey Lopes, traded to Oakland. That made him the first member of the "eternal infield" to be dispatched; it represented a statement of confidence from the Dodger organization about the crop of young ball players in their minor league system, specifically in San Antonio and Albuquerque.

There looked to be a wealth of talent down there in the spring of 1982. Steve Sax would take over for Lopes. Sax had good speed, and had compiled some impressive statistics in Triple A, including a league-leading batting average of .346. Two pitchers had seen service with the Dodgers in 1981 and seemed ready for fulltime duty in '82—Tom Niedenfuer and Alejandro Pena. There were two other promising youngsters who seemed destined for big-league futures—Greg Brock and Mike Marshall—both, interestingly enough, first basemen.

Which brings me to the second question: What about the future of Steve Garvey in Los Angeles? I honestly did not know.

There was no contact from the Dodgers after the World Series, and nothing in those early weeks of spring training, when everybody was working so hard to get ready for the opening of the Grapefruit League schedule.

Even though my contract ran through the 1982 season, I very much wanted to get it all settled before opening day. I knew what was going to happen if we didn't. People had already started asking, and that was going to continue to build. Fans, the press, everybody asking the same question.

My fantasy was that Peter O'Malley would come up to me one morning while I was getting dressed and say, "Listen, Steve, you've been a member of the Dodger family for all these years, there is no way we're going to let you get away. You're one of us. We appreciate the way you've conducted yourself, in good times and bad. Right now they are drawing up a contract that is going to bind you to the team forever, for the rest of your playing days and even after. Here's my hand on that."

But that never happened. All I got was stalling. As the spring progressed and we worked our way through the schedule, each new batch of reporters came at me with the same questions: Have the Dodgers contacted you? What do you think's going to happen? Are you going to be playing for Los Angeles in 1983?

All I ever got out of the organization was that conversation with O'Malley at the little airport near training camp: two cars, meeting out in the middle of the deserted tarmac. It probably looked like one of us was buying top-secret defense plans. The only thing being sold that day was blind trust. Have faith in the Dodgers and tell the press no comment. That was all Peter said, and then he drove off.

After twelve years of establishing an open policy with the press—a policy, incidently, actively supported by the organization—he wanted me to clam up. I couldn't. But neither did I have anything of substance to say.

The season didn't start off as well as I thought it would, and very quickly some people got nervous.

Repeating as world champions is really difficult, especially today. Look how few teams are able to pull it off. There is so much at stake, and so much talent out there ready to knock you off. But the tension around the Dodgers, even before the season opened, was excessive. The players weren't the source—management was.

They got it into their heads that we were complacent. Believe me, one championship gained, after courting so much disaster, doesn't leave you complacent. But management was convinced, and fought to stamp out our supposed complacency. The work program was picked up, to sweat it out of us. All they succeeded in doing was making us tired for the regular season.

We opened up by winning our first two games at home against San Francisco, then split two with San Diego and two on the road at Houston. Then we dropped the next six in a row. The tension was so bad you could hardly breathe.

Lasorda took me out of my usual fourth spot in the batting order and moved me to second. I couldn't believe I was moved from a position where I had been so successful for so long, and so quickly after winning a championship. We were a proven commodity—why mess with us?

Second is not my best position. Your responsibility there is to get on base, to take a pitch for a guy who can potentially steal. It's a place where you've got to be selective, to work out a walk and be a table-setter for the guys batting third and fourth. I don't walk much because I'm aggressive at the plate. That's how I've survived in the major leagues all these years. That's how I've prospered, and in part how the Dodgers have prospered.

Then they moved me to sixth. They moved me to seventh, and then to fifth. I don't like to use the word panic, but a strong current of anxiety emanated from the decision-making apparatus of the Dodgers.

Atlanta started off like a rocket, winning their first thirteen games. Fourteen games into the season, we trailed them by seven, and spent the first one hundred games lodged in third place. It got to a point where I didn't even get mad at Lasorda's shifting me around, because it was so ridiculous. And I was beginning to get the sense that the batting order wasn't always his decision, that he was being influenced by upper management. Regardless, I couldn't control that situation. I tried to keep up my average, hit a few home runs, and help the team as much as I could.

But the pressure was getting to me. The season was shaping up as my worst since I took over at first base in 1973. As we rolled into May my average had fallen to below .230. One Sunday game against Montreal, Lasorda even sat me down in favor of Rick Monday. In 253 games, that was the first time I didn't start. He brought me in the fifth to pinch-hit, keeping my streak alive at 968 games. I struck out; we lost, 13–1.

It was June before there was any direct contact with the Dodgers concerning my future. Al Campanis called Jerry Kapstein at the end of a road trip, and we all met at Dodger Stadium. It was Campanis, vice-president in charge of player personnel;

Dodger president Peter O'Malley; executive vice-president Fred Claire; Jerry; and me. The tone of the meeting was that they definitely "had an interest" in signing me for the following season, but it was their thought that it was best to negotiate after the season.

I explained my situation, how I was being hounded daily by the press. They repeated that "No comment" was the best position. All I wanted was for them to tell me they were going to sign me, and the details could be worked out later. I just wanted to get it settled, to put it out of my mind so I could get back to playing baseball. They said they couldn't do that. They said they didn't know whether they were going to sign me or not.

That was a blow. I felt this queasiness inside, like someone had kicked the wind out of me. I looked at Jerry and he looked at me. Neither of us showed any emotion, but we knew things looked bad.

That was probably the first moment it was clear this wasn't some huge misunderstanding, a problem to be solved by sitting down and talking it through. Sure, the Dodgers had a policy of not negotiating before the contract was up, but that was for somebody else. Not for me. That just wasn't the way this scenario was supposed to work out.

I've talked before about the business of maturing. This was a crucial year in that process. This time I was not learning new material, but learning to recognize and accept old material.

While the Dodger organization has always been one of the best run in all of athletics, they had done several things over the years that had troubled me. That is the way in any relationship; one accepts minor transgressions. The key is to know in your heart what is minor and what is not.

With *Inside Sports*, I had asked them to support me when I sued, to make a statement against the magazine. They said their lawyer suggested they not do that.

When I was having all that trouble with the woman who was harassing me and bothering Cyndy and the girls, I went to the Dodgers for help. O'Malley wondered if paying her off wasn't the best approach. Give her $5,000, $10,000 to go away. Can you imagine paying off every crazy who comes along?

It just seemed the Dodgers have a feel for the public's perception, like finding a place in the organization for a Don Newcombe or a Maury Wills after they'd had trouble with alcohol or drugs, or, in my case, having all the students from Garvey Junior High come free to a game. They still do that, even after I've left.

But the other stuff, the quiet support for players still active, that wasn't there. Or those little gestures that say this club has feelings more genuine than might come from a public relations department—they were so often missing.

When Dixie Walker died in 1982, I waited for some announcement on the Diamond Vision, or for the flag to be lowered to half staff. Something. Some statement that this was a man who had been an integral part of Dodger history. But nothing came.

Maybe there was a political issue I didn't understand. Maybe Dixie still carried a stigma from the Jackie Robinson controversy, or in some other way fell out of grace. I approached Fred Claire and he said he just hadn't thought about it. Or maybe it wasn't that important. If that was the thinking, it's wrong. It's especially wrong in an organization that fosters the kind of family image that the Dodgers have had all these years, with their emphasis on tradition, with Dodgertown streets named Roy Campanella Drive and Sandy Koufax Lane. If you're going to create that image, you've got to have continuity behind it.

My sense of what it meant to be a Dodger was formed very suddenly, at the age of seven. At the first sight of Reese and Robinson and Hodges and Campanella—and even more, as I got to know them, to play catch with them, to talk with them—I became infatuated with the idea of becoming a ballplayer.

And not just any ballplayer—a Dodger. And as I watched these heroes of mine, watched them sign autographs, chat with fans, joke with their teammates, I formulated what I thought a major-leaguer should be, and what a life in baseball meant. Surely nothing could be better than that life. And, from what I could see, the rules that led to success were not so complicated:

1. Work hard at learning your craft—train and practice.
2. Be a friend to your teammates; that's what a teammate is.
3. Support the ball club, for the club is authority.
4. Give to the fans, because it is for their entertainment that you play.

I'm not saying that I actually had a list to follow. But I was pretty observant, even back then. There was nothing I liked better than watching the Dodgers, and learning from what I saw. I watched other teams, too. Cincinnati, and St. Louis; Pittsburgh and Detroit. There was a difference between them and the Dodgers, a way of behaving, of carrying themselves.

When I grew up I learned the difference between class and style. Everybody's got a style; there's good style and bad style, flash and substance. But class is something else. Class is an elevated manner in all things.

My Dodgers had class, in dealing with their teammates and the fans, and in the game itself. From what I saw in them evolved an attitude of what a successful baseball player should be. And since that was what I wanted to be more than anything else, it was that attitude I strived to emulate.

For a while, it seemed to be working. For nearly twenty years. But somehow, along the road to becoming successful and popular, I managed to alienate my teammates, fail in my marriage, and, finally, even be rejected by the team I worked so hard to serve. Someone was sending me a message: My plan was flawed.

Actually, only my vision was flawed. As I grew and matured and worked hard to become the ball player I always dreamed of, I never fully grasped that my original fantasy was based on the perception of a seven-year-old boy. I saw only good: Big, strong men in their glory, living out the myth of endless childhood. And whatever acts of kindness and bravery I did not actually see, my imagination could supply. These were my heroes, and they could do no wrong.

I wasn't even seeing them in their real world, in the final days of a pennant drive, when the long schedule had beaten their bodies and the pressure of winning and losing had robbed them of their civility. That was spring training, when everybody is loose and happy, rested from a winter off and eager to get back to the game they love. For everyone in baseball, spring training is the best of possible times.

Somewhere in a subliminal level of my mind, I suppose, I was aware of this fault in my perfect picture. Even back in 1956, being on a baseball team was not the same as having twenty-four brothers, the organization was not a substitute parent, and signing autographs and visiting sick kids was not what ball players did in their spare time, except maybe in the movies. But it was a nice picture, a comfortable picture for me to live with. And as the years passed and my dreams began to be realized, I saw no reason to challenge it.

Once things began to fall apart and I was forced to look at my life and how I was living it, I think it was just too late to do anything about it. I was what I had become. And, upon close examination, while some of the bloom was gone, I wasn't too unhappy with that. I still believe in those basic attitudes—in that original set of rules—in theory and practice.

It might have been helpful for me and everyone around me had I realized that all things are absolute in the mind of a seven year old. I probably was not seeing what I thought I was seeing in those early spring training camps. Some of the old Dodgers might have been wonderful, but not all. And certainly, not to the extent that I perceived.

And just as the Dodgers I saw getting off the plane in 1956 were not the Knights of the Round Table, neither was the organization for which they played an extended nuclear family. It was and is a business operation, and, like most businesses, efficient often to the point of being heartless.

The Dodgers have earned a reputation for "good timing" when it comes to their athletes. They were the team known for trading a player a year or two early, when the man still had some market value. That's called good business in baseball; nobody takes it personally. But by 1982, when that business sense involved me and the players around me, it became very personal.

My situation with the Dodgers said more than just what they felt about me. It was a window to the future. They had gotten rid of Davey Lopes. I was surely on shaky ground. Could Ron Cey not be next? We all had come up through the organization, had established ourselves in the time when free agency was greatly escalating the pay scale in baseball. In other words, we were all making a lot of money, and, in the Dodgers' eyes, were approaching the end of our careers. It was time, they felt, to turn to the kids in San Antonio and Albuquerque.

Dusty Baker had signed a lucrative, five-year contract prior to the 1981 season, one that gave him the right to block any trade he did not like. Not long after that, the Dodgers began their youth movement, and soon it came time to cut Dusty loose. They began shopping him around, and eventually worked out a deal with Oakland.

But Dusty blocked it. Suddenly stories began to surface about his taking drugs, about his being involved with people selling drugs. I never believed it. I'd known Dusty far too long. When you hit behind somebody in the lineup, year after year, a special kind of communication develops. Some of it is spoken, some un-spoken. He was a man I could depend on, a man I could trust. And he was a man I felt was not involved with drugs. Pure and simple, he was being maligned, discredited as a ball player. The question is who would be doing it, and why? There were a lot of stories, leaked from someplace.

Obviously, someone was angry at Dusty. Someone wanted to punish him with the only tool available, by blackballing him from baseball. I'm sorry to say that is an old trick in this game.

To a certain extent, it worked here. The Dodgers released Dusty after the 1983 season. As hard as I tried, I could not get the Padres interested. They would have signed him in a minute if it hadn't been for the drug rumors—Ballard Smith of the Padres told me as much—but they wouldn't touch him.

Johnnie B. (Dusty) Baker, Jr., big, strong, hard-hitting out-fielder with Los Angeles from 1976 through 1983; released in February of 1984 and signed with Giants; now with Oakland A's:

"It started early on in my contract; I think Garv was still with the team. Somebody leaked that I was involved with drugs. That I was taking drugs; that I was selling drugs. It was rumored, by a 'confi-dential, reliable source.'

"I wasn't taking drugs. I wasn't selling drugs. I'm not a stupid person.

"They had tried to trade me to Oakland, and I refused because I didn't like the terms. Only then did the rumors begin. I don't know who put them out; I can't say. I don't want to get into a lawsuit. I had to sign a special waiver saying I wouldn't sue the Dodgers for slander.

"Why should I have to sign that, just to be able to play baseball?

"When all this happened, Gary Matthews and Garv defended me the best of anybody. A lot of guys were afraid to come out and speak because they were afraid of losing their Mercedes. Not Garv. He said

he would stake his reputation on me. I know he tried to get me to San Diego.

"Garv and I go back a long way. We very rarely went out to dinner. We rarely went out at all. But we had a mutual understanding. A respect."

The first time the Dodgers made an offer was late in July, while the team was on the road. They called Jerry and he called me. It ended up not being what we wanted to hear. The money wasn't right, but the big problem was time. We wanted a five-year contract, something that would see me to the end of my career. They wouldn't offer more than three years.

But at least there was something, something we could work with. At least they wanted to make an offer. I so much wanted to get the whole thing straightened out.

It was about then that the team seemed to wake up. We were ten games out, and I was still hitting down in the order—fifth, sixth. I made a suggestion to Tom that he bat me where I had been most successful. He said he'd think about it. He put me back to fourth, and we started to win. We swept the Braves, won two of three in Cincinnati, then came back to Dodger Stadium and took another four from Atlanta and three from the Reds. Suddenly we were in first place by a half game.

We battled back and forth with Atlanta all through August and September, leading by as many as three games, falling behind by three. All that time Jerry was in contact with the Dodgers, but the nature of the talks was disheartening. First they wouldn't go to five years. We had to reduce our years. We had to reduce the amount of money and change some of the language, the details of the contract. It seemed like all we were doing was giving.

I got angry. After all I had been through with the Dodgers, they were talking to me as if they were paying me by the hit. That wasn't the way it was supposed to be. Those were tense months, and the pressure was getting to all of us.

Toward the end of September, leading the Braves by three games, we proceeded to lose eight straight. Lasorda had a meeting eight straight nights. He tried to motivate us; he tried to yell at us; he tried pleading. But everybody had heard all his stories, knew all his tactics. What we really needed was to win a ball game. We couldn't.

There was one night—I don't even remember who we were playing—when we trailed in the ninth by one run. Cey was on first and I was up. I looked at Danny Ozark, the coach flashing signs, but I didn't see the hit and run. Cey took off and I took a pitch low and away as the catcher threw Ron out. I singled on the next pitch, but they got us out and we lost another game.

I came into the clubhouse and Lasorda started yelling at me. "How the hell could you miss that hit-and-run sign? What're you trying to do? You better bear down more than that!" I just stood there and listened to him, until he marched back to his office.

The next day he called me into the runway that leads to the dugout and apologized. He said he was sorry, that he just lost it, and I told him I was sorry I'd missed the sign. That conversation took place in private; the screaming was in front of my twenty-four teammates. Even the usually jolly Lasorda was showing signs of wear under the prolonged strain.

That's the way it was during those last weeks. We were one back on the last day, playing at San Francisco. Down the coast, Atlanta was playing San Diego. The scoreboard kept us informed. We were tied 2–2 in the fifth inning while the Padres led the Braves 5–1. But in the seventh, Joe Morgan, playing in his last game, hit a two-run homer and it was over.

I remember my last at-bat. The count was 2 and 2, and Greg Minton threw me a slider, low and away. I'm still sure in my heart it was a ball—it was at least a ball's width outside—but Dutch Rennert called it a strike. Strike three.

Walking back to the bench, I looked up to the box seats above our dugout. There was Peter O'Malley, sitting with Al Campanis, and they were expressionless. There was no sign of life. Jerry Kapstein was there, sitting about ten rows up on the rail with Bob Jones, a friend of ours from San Diego. Jerry gave me a kind of "hang in there" smile.

I was the last one in the locker room that afternoon. The last one to take off his uniform. I was not eager. I just sat there, talking to some of the reporters, and thinking about it all; about the game, about all the games.

In my first time up for the Dodgers, thirteen years before, I had struck out. There was a good possibility that my last at-bat would be a strikeout. Bookends, around my career in Dodger blue.

17

Jerry and the Dodgers had several conversations during the last two months of the season, but the serious negotiations did not begin until after that final game with the Giants.

I would like to say that I still held some optimism, but my feelings could not help being affected by the events of that year. When people don't communicate with you, you get a feeling that you're not wanted very badly. At the very least, I would have to say that their not making any offer until July 29 was an indication of a split in opinion within the Dodger organization. It is not unreasonable to speculate that while some factions wanted me there for 1983 and beyond, others did not, and would have preferred not to offer any contract at all. They felt, apparently, that Greg Brock was ready to take over first base, and that I was expendable.

This is not purely my own supposition; the newspapers and television were full of the controversy. A lot of people were speculating about what was going on, and what the outcome would be. I would have had to be very naïve to feel confident about my future as a Dodger.

Joe Morgan ended our season on Sunday afternoon. Two days later at Dodger Stadium O'Malley, Campanis, Bob Walker, the Dodger lawyer, and Jerry met. They met again two weeks later, and then on the following Monday. One week later—on November 3, a Wednesday—they met from 2 in the afternoon till nearly 1 o'clock in the morning. The same group met again on Thursday.

That was the week of my Sports Classic for the MS Society—two days of tennis, racquetball, a five- and a ten-kilometer run. It was necessary that I spend a certain amount of time down in the San Fernando Valley where it was all happening. This was my project, then in its eighth year.

While those events are always pretty well covered by the press—we have a lot of celebrities—they were particularly well attended that year, with most of the questions centering on the Dodgers and my contract. The deadline for signing with the Dodgers was November 6 at midnight, New York time. That's 9 P.M. in Los Angeles. If the team and I could not sign a contract by then, I automatically became a free agent, allowed to sell my talents on the open market.

Up until that deadline, I could sign only with Los Angeles. After 9 on the 6th, I could sign with nobody—including L.A.— until after the reentry draft, scheduled for the following week. Only with those teams that selected me in the draft could I negotiate.

November 6 was a Saturday. I spent the day at the Mid-Valley Racquetball Club, where the racquetball portion of the Sports Classic was held. Jerry spent the day negotiating with O'Malley,

Campanis and Walker at the law offices of Paul, Hastings, Jan-
ofsky and Walker in downtown Los Angeles. The Dodgers had
begun their talks by offering a three-year contract worth $1 mil-
lion a year; we were looking toward five years, at $1.5 million a
year. By Saturday we were closer to agreement than that, but still
far apart.

At 2:30 in the afternoon, Jerry went into their offices, which
are on two floors in one of the Arco Towers. When he reached the
final stages he was to call for me. A good friend of his, Jerry
Boyd, who happens to be police chief of Coronado, was off duty
that day, and offered to stay in touch with Kapstein through the
radio in his car. Jerry Boyd picked me up at the racquetball club
at about 6 P.M.

The Dodgers' final offer at that point was $5 million for four
years. That sounds like a lot of money, and of course it is. But we
had been in that situation in 1977—having negotiated a contract
that was lucrative when signed. I was one of baseball's highest-
paid athletes in 1977; midway through that contract I became
underpaid.

There are two ways that an athlete can deal with such a situation during the term of his contract. He can accept it and go on
playing, or he can go in and demand that the contract be re-
negotiated. The latter is something I was not comfortable doing,
and Jerry agreed. It is his feeling—with all of his clients—that
you bargain as hard as you can for the best possible contract at
the time and then you honor it.

Of course the club can always admit that conditions have
changed, call in the player and offer to extend his contract at a
new and higher figure, effective from that season on. I guess we
were hoping the Dodgers would do that around '79 or '80, but
they didn't. It was not our place to suggest it. At the very least,
you hope the club will see the relative injustice of the old contract—and possibly even appreciate the athlete's continuing to

honor it—and respond by making up the difference in the new agreement. Up until the spring of 1982, I felt sure this would happen.

The last option for the athlete and his agent is to make certain that a new contract does not leave him in the same situation as did the old one. By then you know the club is not going to voluntarily adjust any inequity, so you had better make sure you aren't caught again. That was what we were trying to do during those long negotiations, and even in the last hour.

We got to 8:45. Final offers had to be made. There was some question about who would go first; Jerry suggested each of us enter our final offer simultaneously. O'Malley didn't like that idea. He said his final offer was $5 million for four years—no incentive clauses, no ancillary addendums of any kind. We said we drew the line at $6 million for four years.

There was a silence that seemed to last for twenty minutes; I'm sure it wasn't more than five or six seconds. Someone—Campanis or O'Malley, I can't recall who—asked if that was it. Jerry said that was as far as we could go. It was 8:53.

There was another silence. Jerry and I stood up, and the other side stood up. Then we walked out. It was finished. I had a hollow feeling. You talk about your whole life—this had been my whole life. The Dodgers were everything I knew.

There was an office next door they had provided for our use. We sat for a few minutes, talking about what had happened. We didn't say much. Mostly we just sat.

In about ten minutes there was a knock. It was Steve Brener, the Dodger publicity director, who had sat in on the final stages of negotiations. He said there was a press conference scheduled for upstairs. We told him we needed more time.

When he walked out, he left the door open, and a few minutes later Al Campanis came in. He shook both of our hands, and he told Jerry how sorry he was that things hadn't worked out. "I was sure they were going to work out," he kept saying.

Then he turned back to me. He thanked me for my service to the Dodgers, and told me how fond he had always been of me. It was a sincere and touching gesture. He paused at the door, said something about giving it their best shot, then he put his hands up, shrugged, and walked out.

Jerry and I sat back down and tried to relax before the press conference. We knew there were going to be a lot of questions. At that moment, neither of us was ready.

Jeremy A. Kapstein, graduate of Harvard College and Boston College Law School, veteran of the U.S. Navy, where he served as a judge advocate, prosecuting attorney, and federal military judge; a sports agent since representing Bobby Grich and Carlton Fisk in 1972; now represents thirty-three professional athletes:

"When we were dealing with the Dodgers for that 1977 contract, while the negotiations were hard and long, there was no doubt that the Dodgers had Steve in their plans for the near and intermediate term. There was no doubt that he was going to be their first baseman.

"During the early negotiations in 1982, I did not get the same feeling. All through that season, I had seen the wear and the tension in Steve. It showed on his face; it showed in his performance on the field. I kept telling the Dodgers, this has taken a heavy toll. 'Don't make the mistake of thinking his productive years as a ball player are over.' That pressure seemed to build all season, and concentrate on that last series in San Francisco. I wanted to be there with him.

"That last game was so strange; everyone seemed to know what was happening, that it could be Steve's last game as a Dodger. Even the press was walking lightly. Before the game, he tried to make the day as usual as possible. Batting practice, infield practice—he went

through it all just as he had a thousand times before. He even borrowed change to call a sick youngster, a friend of Bob Jones.

"After the game, I got permission to be with Steve in the clubhouse. He stood by his locker, answering the questions of the reporters. They weren't only the local press—sportswriters had come from all over the country. But they were so restrained, asking their questions with an unusual gentleness, some just wanting to offer him luck.

"Players, in various stages of getting dressed, stopped by the locker. Dusty Baker. Steve Sax. A few others. They didn't say much; some just put a hand on his shoulder, then moved on. When they had all left, Steve sat down on the little stool in front of his locker. There was an air of disbelief to the scene, as he sat there, talking to me about his life with the Dodgers—all those years coming down to that afternoon.

"He looked down at the uniform, and there were tears in his eyes. He turned to me and said, 'Jer, I don't want to take this uniform off. I can't believe this is happening.' ·

"But it was happening. And as intimate as those moments were, as personal as were the feelings, as we moved through the weeks that followed it became clear that everybody in the city was involved. That was something none of us expected. Everybody seemed to care.

"The news coverage built, day after day. Reporters were always waiting at the Dodger offices—sometimes, during the last week, twenty and thirty of them. There were demonstrations; a group of Girl Scouts went to Dodger Stadium in the rain one day with a sign pleading with the team to sign Steve before the draft. It was during that period, from October 1 till November 6, that the negotiations changed tone. During those weeks, I really felt that Peter O'Malley wanted to sign Steve. I hadn't always been so sure.

"During those last weeks, I kept telling Steve I expected the Dodgers to make a big move at the end. Right up until 8:53 on Saturday, I just felt it was going to work out. But I was wrong."

After the press conference—there must have been forty or fifty reporters, with hot lights, television cameras, microphones—

Jerry and I went to the Calabasas Inn for something to eat. It's one of my favorite places, and they gave us a nice private table off the lounge.

We ordered, but just kind of picked at our food. There was a television set up over the bar. I don't remember the program, but they had been running bulletins along the bottom of the screen all evening. As we sat there we saw: "Steve Garvey failed to come to an agreement with the Dodgers and will become a free agent. Details at 11."

When the news came on, the bartender kept switching stations, catching each broadcast as they covered the press conference. It was very strange, sitting there and watching that. In the restaurant, the mood was strange, as people kept coming up to thank me, to wish me luck, to ask me why.

It was after midnight when I got home that night. I was worn out, emotionally drained. I felt nothing—no sadness, no anger. Nothing.

As I got ready for bed in the empty house, it began to hit me that the most important period of my life had come to a close. By then Cyndy and I had decided to get a divorce. And now my relationship with the Dodgers had ended.

As numb as I felt that night, I don't think that having Cyndy and the girls home waiting for me would have made me feel any better. Even if everything else in my life had been perfect, the team had been so much a part of my identity over the years, that I couldn't help but feel completely empty. It's not like retirement, or a special achievement—things you want to share with the people you love. This was a separation from something that I had grown so close to that, in my mind—in my heart—the Dodgers and I had become one. Just as no one else can understand that relationship, neither can anyone else understand what happens when it ends.

You would have had to be there, all the way through. To pick up the bats for Gil Hodges, Jim Gilliam. To almost get hit in the head as the sun sets in center field in Ogden, Utah, in early August, batting against a right-handed sidearm pitcher. To be on the throwing end of a ball that bounces in the dirt for your 28th error in 1972, then circle the bases in the fourth game of the '74 playoffs with your first home run with the whole nation watching. You'd have to have stayed in the old Navy barracks in Dodgertown in March when the air smells of orange blossoms and you sneeze your head off, gotten knocked down in the batting cage by Iron Mike, the mechanical pitching machine, when it wasn't quite adjusted.

And all that as a Dodger—my whole life as a Dodger. I thought that would go on forever; I wanted it to. Staying with one team throughout my whole career was important to me. The Musials had done it; the Kalines; the Yastrzemskis. When you have a dream like that, and it ends, the feeling is loss, in its most profound sense, like losing yourself. No one can understand that. Trying, regardless how well meaning the effort, is almost an intrusion.

I guess I am saying I was better off being alone that night. Because I was alone.

When I was able to take a step back and think about the experience, and try and understand why it happened, several things occurred to me. Certainly part of it was simple economics. I was nearly thirty-four, and, in the Dodgers' eyes, on the downside of my career. Their desire to commit only to a three-year contract said they did not want to be saddled with an aging ballplayer making over one million dollars a year. Especially when they had a Greg Brock waiting in the wings.

But something else was going on, something not reflected in salaries, contracts and depth charts. There is a Dodger philosophy that says "No individual player is that important; it's the name 'Dodger' that sells." I first heard it verbalized by Danny Goodman, who was head of advertising and novelties for the Dodgers until he died in 1983. He meant that no player was bigger than the team. You think of the Cincinnati Reds of the 1970s and most people think of Pete Rose or Johnny Bench; mention the Phillies who won in 1980, it's Mike Schmidt. You say Dodgers, they want you to think DODGERS.

The real challenge to that in modern times came when Sandy Koufax was there, and then Koufax and Drysdale. Their joint holdout in that salary dispute was saying "We're big enough to do this—you need us." The Dodgers fought hard, and won.

Over the years I became someone who, possibly more than any other player in a long time, symbolized the Dodgers. First, I had a connection with the old Brooklyn Dodgers, something that I felt strongly. I had come up through their system, and had always worked hard to carry the name Dodger proudly out into the community. The result was that when people thought of the Dodgers, they thought of Steve Garvey, and vice versa. It was as if I had a slightly longer name: Steve Garvey of the Dodgers. I liked that, and I lived my life in such a way that that association was perpetuated.

For a long time, the organization liked it, too. They always knew they could count on me to represent the club and baseball in the best possible light. I remember Davey Lopes calling me a "walking public relations department." He did not intend to compliment me, but he wasn't far from the truth. And the organization approved.

But at some point that became a problem for them. I was becoming a threat to that old Danny Goodman philosophy. And when I demanded a contract that I thought was fair instead of accepting their idea of fair, that was too much. I was dismissed, proving, in their eyes, the philosophy: No player is that important; they can get along without anyone. I guess they can.

Most of this insight has come lately. Then, I had little perspective on the situation. Even in the days following that Saturday meeting, I clung to the idea of remaining a Dodger. They had no such plan. They had made it clear that those negotiations were *it*, that they had no intention of selecting me in the reentry draft. That was their policy, they said. (Since then, they have changed, drafting Bill Russell in 1984 and then re-signing him.) Neither, however, would they receive another player in the process of turning me loose. Usually when a player of my calibre—called a Type A Player—is drafted, his former team is entitled to compensation by selecting an "unprotected" player from any team signing up for the draft. But my age made me an exception. Players who have twelve years of service or are going through reentry for a second time require only an amateur draft pick for compensation.

Nine teams were interested in my services: the Yankees, Pittsburgh, San Francisco, Seattle, Texas, Houston, the Cubs and White Sox, and the San Diego Padres.

Even before the draft, I had some thoughts about where I might like to play. San Francisco was a possibility, as was San Diego. I thought it might be interesting to play in New York or Chicago; I had always enjoyed big cities.

If it was possible, I wanted to stay in the National League. The consecutive-game playing streak—then at 1,107 games—was very important to me. I knew I had no chance of catching Lou Gehrig, but Billy Williams' National League record of 1,117 was within easy reach.

Jerry had talked with several clubs while we were still negotiating with the Dodgers. You can do that, so long as you don't discuss money.

Soon after the draft he and I took a little trip. We visited San Francisco, then went on to Chicago, New York, Houston, and

San Diego. We didn't visit every team that drafted me. Some, like Seattle and the White Sox, couldn't afford me.

I mostly discussed personality and philosophy; Jerry talked money. By the time I got back to Los Angeles, we knew the main teams were the Giants, the Cubs and the Padres. Those three stayed in pretty close till the end. Within 48 hours of our making the decision to go with San Diego, it could have been any of them. At that point, Ballard Smith, the Padres' president, made an offer that put it over the top. We signed on December 21, one day before my birthday.

The contract was for five years, a total of $6.6 million, plus bonuses that could bring that to $8 or $9 million. In 1984, my being named MVP in the playoffs was worth an extra $150,000. Playing in the All-Star Game was worth $25,000. And there is an attendance clause that could bring as much as $200,000. It was worth only $50,000 in '84, but I can see that improving. San Diego seems to enjoy winning.

It was exactly the kind of contract that I was looking for. And it wasn't just the money. The wording was strong, and the length of time fit my plans for playing. Most important, it said something about my value as an athlete. Not just the number of hits or the runs I could score, but the intangible contributions that I felt I could make to the team and the organization. That was what I was trying to tell Los Angeles, and they didn't want to listen.

Ballard F. Smith, president of the San Diego Padres:

"I was utterly amazed the Dodgers didn't re-sign Steve. It is a testament to their tremendous faith in their ability to generate new talent, and their inability to adjust to the times. Free agency is part of those times. They believe the Dodger way is the only way, and they have developed an arrogance over the years that they can do it better than anybody else. They happen to be wrong about that.

"Though other teams were interested in Steve, there was every reason for him to sign with us. We're in Southern California, near his home. We are a club—and a city—where he could make an impact. This city was ripe for a legitimate sports hero. For our part, we were looking for a superstar who would give us the appearance of respectability.

"But there was more at stake here than appearances. We felt the club was at that point where a Steve Garvey could help us make that final hurdle to becoming a contender. No one expected it to happen as quickly as it did."

18

To say that my first spring training day with the Padres took me back to Vero Beach in 1969 would not be 100 percent true. I came to Dodgertown when I was just twenty, one of a huge crop of rookies known by nobody but a few coaches. In Yuma, Arizona, in 1983, it was a different story.

That first day there were reporters and photographers everywhere. Television crews followed me from calisthenics in the outfield to hitting in the batting cage to first base for infield practice. It seemed the cameras, notebooks and microphones outnumbered the bats and gloves.

I remember Terry Kennedy, the Padres' catcher, looking around in amazement. "Usually," he said, "only the Escondido *Times* would be here."

On the other hand, some things were exactly the same as my very first spring; The stiffness when you stretch to dig a low throw out of the dirt. The sting in your hands before they're toughened to batting. Mostly it's the smells that take you back. The smell of fresh-cut grass when you first walk out onto the field. The smell of baseballs and the smell of powdery resin; the combination of pine tar and resin together, all sticky on the bat.

They are triggers, and they whisk you back. You remember the first time you got liquid pine tar on your hands, how tough it was to get off. The first time I ever touched resin, when I was seven, the smell stayed with me for days. I would fall asleep with my hand close to my pillow so the smell of baseball would fill my head.

The park is different and the people are different, but the senses are the same. The sounds of bat striking ball, the murmur of the crowd. The sight of a ball rotating as it approaches the plate, or a perfect bunt that dies on the grass. You may be fifteen seasons and two thousand miles from your first spring, but those flashes link them.

There is always a bit of anxiety about a new situation, a new training camp, a new part of the country, if only because you don't know where things are. When I checked into the Ramada Inn, I had to ask where the Padres training camp was. When I reached camp, I had to ask where the major league locker room was. For all those years, I never had to think of such things.

But of course this was not Vero Beach, Florida. This was Yuma, Arizona. I called one of the guys in Florida that first week; maybe it was Reuss. I told him I'd found the beach, but was still looking for the ocean.

I knew the guys on the team, though not well. They made my coming there very easy. There was a quality of lightness to the clubhouse that made me feel I was going to be happy there. And while I missed some of my teammates on the Dodgers, it didn't take long to see that this was going to be home. Kurt Bevacqua, kind of an Italian Jay Johnstone, was lockered next to me. Fate had put me beside the Padres' resident flake; I immediately checked my baseball glove for brownies, my shoes and cap and anything else easily booby-trapped.

We opened up at San Francisco, winning a wild one, 16–13. Two weeks later we were in Los Angeles for a weekend series. It was my first trip back to Dodger Stadium. That first game, on Friday night, was the 1,117th consecutive game in which I had played, tying Billy Williams' National League record.

I reached the park about 4 o'clock, an hour before the Padres' team bus was scheduled to arrive. That was the time I had been accustomed to getting there, and old habits are hard to break. What an odd sensation that was, coming to the stadium as the opposition, dressing in the visitors locker room, not wearing Dodger blue.

I was hitting third, and when they made the announcement over the public address system—"Now batting for the Padres, Steve Garvey, first base"—the crowd stood and applauded. And they kept on applauding—52,000 of them. They stood and applauded for two full minutes. I'll never forget that night.

Saturday—the game that broke Williams' record—the Dodgers scheduled a special ceremony before the game. Fred Claire had called me during the spring to ask if that would be all right. I told him of course it was all right—I was honored. I was also very surprised. As I told one Los Angeles reporter, my record for predicting what the Dodgers would do was .000.

The festivities were very touching. Billy Williams was down on the field; my mother and father were there. I got a chance to thank the fans. Again they stood and applauded; of course I cried.

We lost those first two games. Finally, on Sunday, we exploded for nine runs and won, 9–1. It was the kind of weekend that stays with you for a long time, pictures in a blur of images that made up the first half of my 1983.

Cyndy and the girls had been back in Los Angeles for most of the 1982 season; we were separated but living in the same house. In the spring of 1983, she went to New York to join Regis Philbin on a local television show.

During that season, whenever I could get to New York to see Whitney and Krisha, I did. Not only in May, when we were playing the Mets, but anytime there was a space in the schedule that permitted a quick trip in—a Monday off after a series in Pittsburgh, on the way back to San Diego, or even a Thursday off between St. Louis and Chicago. It made for some hectic travel, but it was the only way to see the girls. By the end of July, I was more than a little frayed around the edges.

It just seemed that everything during that period required a maximum effort. First the intensity of the negotiations with the Dodgers, then all the flying and talking in search of a new team. Finding a new place to live in a new city, moving my business and getting relocated, all the while making the flurry of appearances for the Padres.

Once the season began, I very much wanted to do well. More than usual. This was a new team, a new bunch of guys. And I had arrived with great fanfare.

It was going well. Through 99 games I was hitting .294, with 76 runs scored—ten more than in my entire last season in L.A.— 59 RBIs and 14 home runs, all that from a man who usually starts off slowly. In addition to the big weekend in Los Angeles, I collected my 2,000th career hit and drove in my 1,000th career run. All in all, I was well on my way to the kind of season that would have indicated I was not a ball player on the decline.

But I was tired. We had played a ten-game road trip, ending with three in Pittsburgh before an off Thursday to fly home. I flew to New York to see the girls, then caught a Friday morning flight back to San Diego. It was that afternoon that I injured my hand.

The whole thing was quirky. First, the game was a 5 P.M. start because we were playing a doubleheader, making up for a game rained out in April. Second, I should never have gotten on base in that first inning. With Pascual Perez throwing out of the sun the way he was, I couldn't see. Then with the count two balls and two strikes, I swung at a slider to keep from striking out, and ended up topping the ball down the third base line. It was an accidental single.

Seven years—1,207 games. That's how long it lasted. For all those weeks and months, through injuries and slumps, trouble in the clubhouse and sadness at home, I played through it all. Had I played in 100 more games—made it to the 38th game of 1984—I would have matched Everett Scott's 1,307, putting me second behind Lou Gehrig. I never thought Gehrig's 2,130 was realistic; I don't plan on still being in uniform in 1989.

It is hard to put into words what all this meant to me. First, you have to have lived it yourself. But before that, you have to come to it with the background and attitude that make something like that of value. In my house when I was growing up, finishing what you start was a religion. Once that principle is established, and you find yourself in the midst of a streak that lasts 400 or 500 games, 600 then 800—1,000 games—it begins to take on a life of its own. You feed it the way you feed your body. Or, more accurately, your ego. You keep it alive because you must.

Only a Billy Williams can understand this. Only someone who has been through a streak knows how it affects your life.

Billy Leo Williams, outfielder for the Chicago Cubs from 1963 through 1974, when he was traded to Oakland for his final active season; he established the National League record for consecutive games played, 1,117, September 22, 1963, through September 2, 1970; he is now batting coach for Oakland Athletics:

"Every time I approached a new level—Richie Ashburn's 730; Stan Musial's 895—I felt satisfaction, and I looked for the next level. Then at some point I began to play as an individual instead of being part of a team, being less aggressive to insure I kept the streak alive. And from there the pressure started to build, pressure I was putting on myself. I had to be in the lineup every day. I even convinced myself the team could not win without me.

"Finally it got to be too much. I had a monkey on my back and I had to get it off. I needed to get some rest. So I took myself out. I was going to sit on the bench, or stay in the clubhouse. But the tension got so bad I went home in the fifth inning."

I don't think I ever got to the point where I played less aggressively to preserve the streak. It ended, after all, on an aggressive play. But I know what Billy means about how important the streak becomes in your life. It becomes huge, like the sun, with all thinking and logic rotating around it.

It distorts thinking. I may not have changed my style of play to prolong it, but I certainly got into some games where my appearance served the streak more than the team. Pinch-hitting in that 13–1 loss to Montreal in 1982 was one. And there were others; "token appearances," the Hall of Fame historian calls them. I'd had my share.

You do it to feed the streak. Because the streak, like the uniform you wear and the game you play, becomes part of your identity. When it is over—when it dies—part of you dies with it. And you mourn.

Those first weeks after the operation were very strange. I was thirty-four years old; I was seventeen when last a summer of baseball went on without me. For most of that time, my life had revolved around a 162-game schedule. Suddenly, it stopped.

I have a place in Deer Valley, Utah, and I went up there for three or four days of relaxation. Hiking, collecting my thoughts, looking back and looking ahead. It was also a chance to see the girls when they were out of school; we went to Hawaii for five days. I got back to Deer Valley later in the summer, this time with my parents. My dad had just retired from Greyhound, and that was a good time to discuss their joining me in San Diego.

I was finding that the end of the streak provided a natural punctuation mark in my life. Not just *period,* the streak is over, now let's get on to the next thing. It was far more complicated. I was being provided with a time to regroup, my first such opportunity in years.

The streak had been an extension of my life as a Dodger. Though I no longer played for Los Angeles, the changeover had happened so quickly, in such a maelstrom of activity, that I had no time to absorb it. Breaking the record in Dodger Stadium, before those fans who I still considered my fans, only cemented that connection. In my heart, I was still a Dodger.

But kneeling there at home plate in Jack Murphy Stadium, the connection was finally broken. I was a Dodger no more.

The first thing I decided was that I did not want to sever my ties with the city of Los Angeles. Too much of me was there. I had matured there. I arrived there at twenty-one, a young man out of college, still in many ways a kid. Those people accepted me, stuck with me through some lean years. I didn't want them to think my affections for them were tied to the salary being paid by the Dodgers. I was going to do everything I could to defeat their baseball team, but I wanted them to know I still loved them.

The Sports Classic for Multiple Sclerosis, the golf tournaments, the charity dinners—I've kept them all in Los Angeles. I still do public service announcements, on radio and television. I still have a house there. At the same time, I was trying to make a new life in San Diego.

By July 1983, I was just starting to understand the city, who the people were who made the decisions, and I could see that I could do much more than I ever could for Los Angeles, simply because San Diego's so much smaller. The key was to become part of the community so the people could see I was not taking their money and running. I first found a place to live, and then went about starting to build a business.

Up until then, most of my business interests were focused around me, personally. Over the years I had assembled an outstanding support group. Jerry Kapstein was my agent. Jim Harper, my business manager, handled all financial matters. Mike Gursey, my personal manager, was in charge of advertising and commercial projects. Norm Brokow of the William Morris Agency advised on radio and television ventures. Alan Rothenberg was my attorney. I kept a small office in Calabases, staffed by Priscella Sellery. My sports classic was run through there.

But the San Diego contract put me at a new level professionally, and gave me a chance to try an idea I had been nurturing for several years. I wanted to begin a marketing company that could commercially merge the connections I had made in business and sports. The plan was to use athletes in marketing projects and services. Companies are always looking for ways to distinguish themselves from their competition; I wanted to use athletes—specifically, athletes known in particular parts of the country to represent business in those areas.

I had an idea and a name—Garvey Marketing Group, or GMG. I needed someone to run it; what I had the least of was time. The job called for someone who had a background in business and finance, but who could apply that to sports. More than someone experienced, I needed someone I could trust. I didn't want to have to worry during the eight months of baseball. More than ever before, at that time in my life, finding someone who would be faithful to me was a major consideration.

There was really only one choice—John Boggs. John's résumé says he was a manager for the business and industrial food service for the Marriott Company and an officer at Riggs National Bank in Washington, D.C. Strip away that polished veneer and you have a baseball junkie. If you call him a *has-been* shortstop, John would beam, because he's really a *never-was*. Good field—no hit.

We met in the Dominican Republic during the winter of 1972. I was down there trying to get my floundering career righted. John was there because of family connections; his grandfather, a resident of the Dominican Republic, had been ambassador to the U.S. during the Roosevelt years. John traveled and played with the Licey team for two weeks. We hit it off immediately, and over the years have become very close.

I had the contacts, both in business and sports, to get projects started. It was going to be John's responsibility to make sure everything worked out, and, eventually, to initiate projects of his own.

Our first project was with McDonald's; Ray Kroc, who began McDonald's, owned the Padres. We got some high-profile ballplayers—like Darryl Strawberry, Gary Carter, and Dusty Baker—to wear wristbands with the McDonald's golden arches, and to make appearances at a Ronald McDonald House. The athletes received $5,000, and McDonald's got ballplayers to draw attention to their charities—and their restaurants.

It was going well until Darryl was on the cover of *Sports Illustrated* with his McDonald wristbands. Chub Feeney, the National League president, saw it and ruled it a commercial use of the uniform. The wristband, of course, is not part of the uniform—never has been. But that effectively ended the project.

We've grown since then, and now represent several athletes on a full-time basis—Steve Sax and Orel Hershiser among them—and have worked through individual deals with several others, including many of the Padres.

While I did a lot of work at GMG when I was on the disabled list, my primary obligation was still to the ball club. With the team itself, it was a little awkward. I had to be visible, but I didn't want to get in the other guys' way. For a ballplayer with a cast on his arm to take up space and draw attention while not contributing is welcomed by nobody. I dressed and attended all home games, making myself available, but usually left before the game was over.

I could do much more for management. Appearances and public relations work, and a few stints doing color on radio broadcasts and tests for their new cable network; and some things of more lasting importance.

Compared to the Dodgers, the Padres were a very young organization, one that had never won. Maturity and success breed quality into an organization, and there were a lot of things that the Dodgers did well that I thought could benefit the Padres. Some were simple and direct: In Yuma the batting cages had pitching machines that had to be hand-fed by a coach, one ball at a time. We had been using automatic-feeding machines in Dodgertown for ten years.

Other things were more complex. On the road, travel schedules are a nightmare—where you stay and how you travel, and when. Some hotels are better than others, more accommodating to teams. Taking charters instead of scheduled flights means a plane is ready when you want to leave, permitting you to take off at midnight instead of getting up to catch an early morning flight.

Some things the Padres were already starting themselves, others not. I found them very receptive. Even to my feelings about their uniforms. Actually, there were two or three of us who collaborated on that effort—Kennedy, Bevacqua, and myself.

When I signed with San Diego, I said that the Dodgers' red, white, and blue uniform made me look like an American flag, and in the Padres' brown, yellow and orange I looked like a taco. It was a joke, but I did think the uniforms were ugly. Basically, they belonged on a softball team.

I've always had a real appreciation for the traditional baseball uniform. I like a top and a bottom that go together, so that there is a symmetry of proportion and line. I like a belt—not an elastic waistband. Out of those efforts came the new Padres uniform: pinstripes, with brown belt and brown shoes. Pinstripes are traditional. And they make you look taller.

Perhaps the most valuable time that summer was spent working on a project called PACE—Professional Athletes Career Enterprises. It is a company whose goal is to help athletes make the transition from sports to the civilian world. Over the years, I had seen too many of my teammates fail to make that move. They lost their money, had their marriages fail, and in some cases ended up with serious alcohol and drug problems.

I had discussed the matter with Rick Talley, a sports columnist for the *Los Angeles Daily News,* and he introduced me to Michael Corey, a friend in the executive search business in Chicago. Corey was interested in the same problem, but from his own end.

At spring training in 1980, Corey and I spent three hours on the porch at Dodgertown, talking about how to cope with the problem. I described the situation as I saw it from my perspective, and he told me how he thought we could approach it in practical terms. Then he went back to Chicago to devise a plan.

Two years later, in the summer of 1982, we opened our doors, using Corey's offices in Barrington, Illinois. Mike contributed his expertise, his financial contacts and his own money; I supplied credibility, and helped draw corporate sponsors, especially Anheuser-Busch, through their vice-president of marketing, Mike Roarty.

The response from all areas of professional sports was excellent; the baseball players' association and the National Basketball

Association both endorsed PACE. But in that first year we discovered that 90 percent of the athletes who became involved were still playing, which meant that we were more involved with testing and evaluating than with placement. Since our profit would come from the hiring companies—a company would pay PACE 30 percent of the first year's salary of the athlete they've hired—we needed to rethink the program.

What we decided in 1983 was to create a separate not-for-profit company to handle all the testing and counseling, a company that could receive grants from corporations and foundations.

That summer the PACE Center for Career Development—or PCCD—was formed. Originally it functioned out of the PACE office, but by 1985 it was part of the GMG headquarters in San Diego. As executive director we hired Ron Stratton away from his job as supervisor of sports marketing at Anheuser-Busch.

The programs are in their infancy, but the early results are encouraging. PCCD has tested and counseled over five hundred athletes, mostly in baseball and basketball. PACE, having purchased the results of that testing from PCCD, has already placed several of those athletes.

It is the potential for assistance that is so exciting. The professional athlete exists in a vacuum. He is courted and looked after from the day the world discovers he has athletic talent, from high school to college to the pros. Along the way most have developed none of the sophisticated skills, such as money management, consistent with the high salaries they command.

When suddenly their careers end, all that support stops. Everyone wanted to help them get into the system, but nobody cares how they exit. We want to help them to leave standing tall and prosper thereafter.

19

To say that spring represents the reawakening of the earth after the frozen sleep of winter may be a cliché, but it's also true. Especially for baseball players. Some actually come south from their homes in the north, leaving snow for the sunshine of spring training. All return to baseball, and to the reawakening of dormant dreams.

My off-season never includes more than recreational winter, but there is always a lot of travel. During the winter of 1983–84, I put on a ski classic in Deer Valley for the Special Olympics, and a golf tournament in San Diego for our Olympic committee. I attended the American Airlines golf tournament in Kona, Hawaii, assumed new duties as the honorary chairman for the United Way in San Diego, had speaking engagements all over the country for Trans-America, McDonald's, Nestlé's and others, and kept up my associations with CHAD and COMBO, the first aiding health agencies and the second the arts in San Diego.

People ask me about all the traveling tiring me out for the season. I do enjoy it. Flying around the country, meeting people and socializing is not painful to me. Too much of it, however, can be draining. But just about the time it starts to get to me, there's spring training. Baseball refreshes me—games and training alike. Especially games. I relax between the lines.

On that March I was more ready for baseball than I had ever been in my life. The cast on my left wrist came off by the end of September, but I never made it back to the active list that season. It didn't seem prudent. I did work hard at getting into shape, and was eager for camp.

There was something very satisfying about the mix of that 1984 team. Changes had been made that gave me the confidence that the San Diego days of being a .500 club were over. Two years in a row they had finished in fourth place, winning and losing 81 games. All but one finish in their fifteen-year history had been worse.

They had signed Goose Gossage as a free agent, and traded to get Carmelo Martinez. Then right before the season started they made a trade to get Graig Nettles. That gave the team an infield of proven veterans with Nettles at third, Garry Templeton at short, me at first, and Kennedy catching. The only question mark was how quickly Alan Wiggins could adapt from the outfield to second base. Every day of spring training he looked better. Everybody felt that Kevin McReynolds in center field was going to be a star, eventually, and Tony Gwynn in right was simply a natural athlete. Martinez in left added power.

It wasn't just the talent that impressed me. It was a kind of psychological blending that's very rare on a team. Everybody seemed to have his place. Even more important, each man at least appeared to be happy with that place. Bringing together twenty-five men with talent is only part of building a winning baseball team. Those men must fit in such a way that the manager can get the most out of each of them. Only then can the whole become more than the sum of its parts, making a team with good talent better than a team of superstars.

The secret of the 1984 team was that egos did not get in the way of players performing at the top of their games. Young and very talented athletes like Gwynn, McReynolds and Wiggins deferred in matters of team leadership to veterans like Nettles, Gossage and myself.

Finally, here was the chance for me to have the kind of involvement with a team that I had always wanted. Call it, if you wish, a contemporary approach to that dream born at spring training with the Dodgers in 1956. Finally, the picture was becoming complete.

The Padres players gave me the opportunity to be the kind of leader that I had always wanted to be on my Dodger teams. Not "leader" as in telling people what to do, but leader by example, leader in teaching. I had learned a lot in my years in the big leagues, learned by experience and by listening to some pretty terrific teachers. All I ever wanted was the chance to pass that along.

Actually, I started to do a little of that while still in Los Angeles. When Steve Sax came up, and Mike Marshall, we spent some good time together. Some of it was just discussing the best places to eat on the road; some was how to lay down a bunt on artificial turf, or how to deal with Mario Soto's change-up, a pitch he throws with a motion identical to his fastball but that travels seven or eight miles an hour slower. It's devastating.

The Book. That's where you can really help a young player. Telling him what the pitcher likes to do in this situation or that, what's his "out pitch," what does he tend to throw late in a game, or does he have a favorite first pitch to me?

The Book's in your head. If you are going to be successful as a hitter, you have to start to keep track of what a pitcher throws, his tendencies, his deliveries, his release point. It is a process you begin as early as possible, in high school and college if you're seeing pitchers often enough—certainly in the minor leagues—so the pattern is already set when you come up. It's just like being a good salesman: You have to know your product, and you have to know the territory. A batter has got to know the pitchers. And he has got to remember.

All those years with the Dodgers, talking to Manny Mota and Dixie Walker, to Dick Allen and Frank Robinson; they all talked situations. What does this pitcher do in this situation? You know, and then you are ready. Like that playoff game in Montreal in 1981. Gullickson had been busting fastballs in all day. So there we were, the game tied in the eighth. I figured he was afraid of feeding me a fastball and would try to start me off with a slider, just to get ahead. He did, and I hit it over the left field wall.

That's what's in The Book. You spend your entire career putting it together, and you want to pass it along. I could tell I was going to get that chance with San Diego. The players were receptive. We had started off that way in 1983, but my season got interrupted. I knew by the spring of 1984 that there was going to be a lot more. It made me feel awfully welcome. It made me feel as if I had found a home.

Timothy Earl (Tim) Flannery, utility player for Padres and senior member of team in terms of uninterrupted service, most of that time wearing uniform Number 6—now Number 11:

"Even before Steve signed with San Diego, I knew he was coming. I just knew. And one day when we were playing the Dodgers and I got to first base, I told him he could have my number.

"When he signed he accepted—Number 6 belonged to him, not me—and he went out and bought me the most expensive suit at Ralph Lauren in San Francisco—$600. It's too nice for me to wear.

"Steve filled a vacuum on this team, a power vacuum. And I don't mean hitting home runs. He seemed to remember everything—how this pitcher pitches, and how to play that batter. But it was more than the things he told us.

"Just having a guy like him in the lineup gives you confidence. You see the way he does the little things that are so big—moving runners from first to second, getting that sacrifice fly in the last inning. And when it comes down to the game situation with the winning run on second and two outs, the guy you want up is Steve.

"Everybody has a role on this club—that's his."

The early part of the 1984 schedule was in our favor. During the entire month of April we had only six games away from home. We won our first four, and at the end of the second week were 10–2, in first place by three games.

Early in May we dropped seven straight. A bunch of the younger players looked at Graig and Goose and me and waited for some reaction. They didn't get any. There was no reason for panic. It was early, and we weren't getting blown out. One game we lost by five runs, but everything else was tight.

That was the hump. When they saw we were under control, they were under control. We started winning again and never stopped.

While we had fallen out of first during our slump, we hadn't dropped from contention. During a thirteen-game homestand in June we moved back into first and never again faltered. By the first of July we led by four games; by the first of August, eight and a half.

There had been no pain in my wrist from the day they removed the cast, but it took me a long time to get my strength back. It wasn't back by the beginning of spring training, and it hadn't returned by opening day, either. I couldn't drive the ball the way I had; I just didn't have the power.

Because I couldn't rely on that power, we as a team had to find a way of winning without my home runs. We did. Alan Wiggins would get on and steal a base, or at least threaten. That gave Tony Gwynn more fastballs, which helped him to the batting championship.

That brought me up many times with men on first and third and nobody out. My job was to hit the ball to the right side. With a man on third and one out, hit the ball up the middle, or even bunt. (I drove in three runs with bunts in the first inning; you can do so many more things when you give up power for control.) It was a pattern that proved to be very successful. While my home run production was the lowest it had been since 1973, I did have fifteen game-winning hits.

The most important thing was that the team was winning. And when you find a formula that results in winning, you don't change it. I got stronger as the season wore on, but we continued to play as we had.

I gave Dick Williams a lot of credit for that. He is too smart a manager to mess with success. That was my second year with Dick, and my respect for him was growing.

In my fifteen years in the major leagues, I've played for three managers. All were very successful, and all very different from one another.

Walter Alston was the dean of the old school, a top manager at a time when discipline on a ball club had a higher priority than it does today. That was before the days of guaranteed contracts and free agency, when a player was bound to a team for the length of his career, or until the team decided otherwise. Management was in total control. Alston spoke and you listened, because he was saying something relevant and pertinent about baseball—that was the only subject being discussed. He knew baseball. But when times were tough—when you were struggling—he didn't have much to sustain you. He probably did, earlier in his career, but he was drained. Over all those years, he'd given whatever he had. ·

Lasorda was more personable, more gregarious. He had known most of those Dodgers in the minors, and had put a lot of time in with them. His approach was more as a psychologist; he tried to motivate on an individual basis. That's very effective when you know the players well, more difficult if the man's new to you. That's why Tom's having more trouble now that the original group has moved on.

I think Dick Williams started off in the Alston school, and is moving more toward the Lasorda school with time. That's good; things have changed. I don't think Walter Alston would be as effective a manager today.

Williams has an astute baseball mind, one in which there are no gray areas. Everything is black or white. He's adamant about staying in the game, mentally, even with a ten-run lead; you never ease up. He's adamant about walks; they're his pet peeve. He is, in his heart, a believer in obeying the rules of how baseball is played. He assumes his players are mature adults who also know those rules. He's more likely to be patient with the younger players, but he figures this is the major leagues. We should all know our jobs.

In terms of being able to motivate players, you would have to list the order as Lasorda, Williams, and Alston. As far as strategy, it's Williams, Alston and Lasorda last.

They were all successful, and they were the most successful when their personalities fit their teams. Sometimes that happens when the organization builds a team around the manager, and sometimes the manager is hired to suit a particular team. But being great means winning over a long period of time. The ultimate test is winning in different situations, even with different organizations. Williams has done that.

The perfect manager today is the one who understands the personalities on his team, and who knows the game well enough to get the most out of his players. That's hard to do now, because the game has changed so much. Money has a lot to do with that. It can be hard to motivate a player with a guaranteed contract, one who no longer must play his best every day to keep his job.

The manager must also placate his superiors. He cannot bench a player making $2 million a year just because he's not performing. The front office wants that man in the lineup.

So on a daily basis, a manager must use positive reinforcement with his men. He must keep working with them, pumping them up, trying to improve their play.

I think Chuck Tanner, now at Houston, does that very well, though he hasn't always had the players to win. Dick Williams is getting to be more and more that kind of manager. No one knows the game better than Dick, and he's beginning to use more positive support. I've seen him change. I've seen him talk to players when they're down, celebrate with them when they win. Look at 1984—it was a three-hug year for Dick and me.

The biggest hug, of course, came after the fourth game of the National League playoffs.

The Cubs had the best record in the league, and were favored in the playoffs, even though we had played them even during the regular season, 6–6. Probably that was a sentimental choice—all those years of Cub frustration.

We opened at Wrigley Field and got blown out, 13–0. Rick Sutcliffe not only pitched a six-hitter, he hit a home run. We came back in the second game and only lost by 4–2.

There was a lot of defeatist talk on the plane ride back to San Diego. Some of the younger guys thought we were out of it. Trailing 2–0 in a seven-game series is one thing; in a five-game series it's quite another. Lose one more and you're finished. I told them we had the Cubs right where we wanted them—fat and confident and going back to our park, where we had come from behind all season. With our fans, it was an ambush.

The plane landed about 9 o'clock that night; buses took us to the stadium to get our luggage. Waiting for us in the parking lot must have been 3,000 people, cheering as the buses drove up. People lining the fences, standing at the entrance, shouting "We'll win it now," and "We're back home now—we'll help." It was something to see.

Two hours before the third game, as the guys ran in the outfield, there were already fans in the park, cheering. Every Padre who came out of the tunnel to run was cheered. It made me think of that final series against Houston in 1980, when the fans at Dodger Stadium got so involved. This time I started gesturing with my arms, urging our fans to get up, to start clapping. They responded. They kept it up through the introductions and all during the game.

We fell behind 1–0 in the second inning, then came alive in the fifth, scoring three runs on the way to a 7–1 win.

The next day, Friday, was off, with only a light workout scheduled. While I was getting dressed at the stadium I began to feel queasy, as if I were coming down with some kind of virus. Then the cramps started. I had some soup for dinner and was in bed by 7 o'clock. All night I was cramped up, pulled into a fetal position. Every couple of hours I'd wake up, soaked with sweat and weak.

By the time I reached the ball park on Saturday I felt a little better. I worked out gingerly—took a few ground balls, a few swings in the batting cage—then lay down in the training room, a towel over my face. I may even have dozed for five or ten minutes. I was still queasy, even a little shaky, for my first at bat, but after that I got more into the game and forgot about my stomach.

We scored two in the third inning on Tony Gwynn's sacrifice fly and my double, but they came back with three in the top of the fourth. We tied it in the fifth when I singled in Tim Flannery, and went ahead with two in the seventh on two walks, my single, and a wild pitch.

The Cubs scored two off Gossage in the eighth to knot the game at 5–5, where it stayed till the bottom of the ninth inning. With one out, Gwynn singled to center, which brought me up for my fifth at bat. You might have one, sometimes two chances in crucial situations in a game. I had already had three, and had either tied the score or put us ahead. As that happens, each time, your confidence builds. You actually get better, physically better. Your timing improves, your aggressiveness builds, your strike zone gets better defined. And the crowd senses what's happening, and they get into it.

As I approached the plate in the ninth they were standing and they were cheering: "Gar-vey! Gar-vey! Gar-vey!" It makes your adrenaline level shoot sky high, but you can't get excited. If you get too aggressive you lose control. You've got to direct all that energy toward hitting the ball.

The first pitch was a fast ball away. The pitcher was Lee Smith. He's about six-six and strong. He tossed to first to check Tony, then stared in at me. Smith lives or dies by power, and I didn't think he was going to fool around with breaking pitches; I don't think he will the next time he faces me, either.

He threw another fastball. I was striding into the pitch and got my arms fully extended. *Crack!* I knew it was gone. I can still see the white ball rising into the semidark background, a halo of light around it.

I remember hitting first base and raising my arm in this euphoric feeling. Everything around me was frozen: the noise was muffled, the movement stopped. Touching second base, I was coming down to earth. I could see the crowd and distinguish voices, though they were a loud echo.

By the time I got to third base, I could see the stands, see the Cubs walking off the field. At home plate our whole team was waiting. Somebody stepped on my heel and my shoe came off. I grabbed it, just as they were picking me up and putting me on their shoulders. When I got to Dick Williams I threw my arms around him. He actually hugged back.

There was no way we were going to lose that fifth game, and it didn't matter that we fell behind 3–0 with Sutcliffe pitching.

It was a hot day in San Diego, and about the sixth inning Rick's ball began to straighten out, lose some of its movement. And his location wasn't as good as it had been earlier. For thirteen consecutive innings he had shut us out; now you could tell, he was losing it.

We loaded the bases on a bunt single to Wiggins, a single by Gwynn and a walk to me. Two runs came home on sacrifice flies by Nettles and Kennedy. It was 3–2, Chicago.

I thought they were going to lift Sutcliffe then, but they left him in. They shouldn't have. We exploded for four runs in the next inning to become the only National League team ever to lose the first two games of the playoff and come back to win.

Winning that series may be the most satisfaction I've known in baseball, considering the circumstances of my coming over from Los Angeles and it being the first pennant for the franchise. And while I do think we *won* the playoffs—rather than Chicago *losing* then—I also think that they let us up. When you win the first two games like that, convincingly, you've got to finish off the other team.

They didn't. They gave us a little room to breathe, and you can't do that with a good team. Once we won the third game, the momentum started to build for us. We used our home field and we used our fans, and we got better and better.

The lesson, once again, is that you can never let up. Never.

In the World Series, there was not much question of momentum. We never really bounced back from the high of the playoffs. Maybe you can pull that off against a team of average ability, but the Detroit Tigers of 1984 were considerably better than average.

And we were hurting. Kevin McReynolds, who hit .300 and drove in four runs in the playoffs, had been a consistent hitter for us all season, broke his hand sliding into second base in the fourth game. And our starting pitching—with the exception of Ed Whitson in the third game of the playoffs—was poor.

Jack Morris pitched a fine game against us in the opener at San Diego, giving up two runs in the first inning and blanking us the rest of the way.

Our moment in the sun—and we weren't there much longer— came in the second game. Whitson gave up three Tiger runs in the first inning, but then Andy Hawkins came in and pitched five and a third shutout innings, with Craig Lefferts finishing. (The Series, and specifically the second game, may have been the turning point in Andy's career; weak as our starters were, the relief corps was magnificent, and he was the best of the lot.) We scored runs in the first and fourth. Then, with one out and two men on in the fifth, Bevacqua came to bat.

It is important to understand something about my friend Kurt. He may be a flake. He may never own a Gold Glove other than the charm he wears around his neck. But the man is a hitter—a smart, aggressive hitter. Sometimes he's too aggressive; he ran us out of an inning in the first game by trying to stretch a double into a triple. But he's enthusiastic, and you like that in a hitter.

In even years the World Series employs the designated hitter rule, normally used only by the American League. In 1984 our DH was Kurt. In the fourth inning he hit a three-run homer, then proceeded to execute a mid-air pirouette on the way to first, clap and raise his hand in the air on the way to second, and blow a kiss to his wife in the stands as he headed for the reception at home.

As I said, he's enthusiastic. And we were even, going to Detroit.

Milt Wilcox and Morris were tough in games three and four. We always seemed one swing away, and never made it. Going into the fifth game, we were down three games to one in their park. That is not exactly a good situation, but we had battled back all season, and all post-season. Coming back, again and again. But that takes its toll.

Detroit went ahead, 3–0, on Kirk Gibson's first inning home run. We scored in the third and fourth to tie, but they pulled ahead in the fifth and iced it with Gibson's second home run in the eighth. From about the sixth inning on you could feel the energy in the crowd begin to take on an unsettling edge. They weren't just happy, sensing a celebration—there was hostility out there.

It made me think of the second game of the 1977 Series, when the fans in Yankee Stadium went crazy in the last two innings, throwing bottles and fruit at our bullpen; a rubber ball thrown from the upper deck hit Reggie Smith in the head.

It's scary. You think of all the positive energy that comes from sports, the cheering and the applauding of people supporting their team. Then you see the dark side of that, the riots at soccer matches, or at our own events. Part of it is surely an expression of economic frustration during hard times, especially in a city like Detroit, where unemployment is high. But the rage surfaces in so many places—not all of them depressed—and is voiced by individuals as well as huge crowds: Fans curse at umpires and fight among themselves; throw missiles at home and visiting players; actually single out athletes for death threats.

Even standing in the middle of all this, I am less frightened for myself than for my society. These are terrifying expressions of anger.

I was in the on-deck circle in the ninth inning with two out and Tony Gwynn up. It was a particularly dark night, and the blaze of lights gave the old stadium a haunting look. Police and guards, arms linked, stood just outside the baselines, braced for the final out. Our families had already been moved from the stands as a precaution, and were aboard their bus outside.

When Tony flied out to left field, the place went wild. Even all those policemen couldn't keep the crowd from rushing onto the field, charging the players and tearing up the turf.

Bad as it was inside, that was nothing compared to the mob outside. Thousands of people yelling and screaming, some of them throwing bottles and cans at our buses. Even the police horses were being hit.

It took us an hour just to creep the six or seven blocks from Tiger Stadium to the expressway. Along the route we saw a burning taxi, and a car turned into a kind of people wagon—people sitting all over it. Bottles were crashing against the bus, bouncing off the roof. The police on board told us to put our coats up against the windows for protection.

It was a long hour, and my mind was not always on the health of society. While we were inside this great big bus, and there were police, nobody felt safe. You began to wonder, just what would it take for them to seriously attack the bus.

We were all very glad to get onto the expressway. And while it took a while to loosen up on the plane, once we were in the air the ride home began to be fun. Lots of talking, lots of singing. There was even dancing in the aisles. We had been to the World Series. We had lost, but we had had a great season. There was some talk, especially among the younger players, that winning the playoffs was really the tough thing, and that taking the Series would have been gravy.

We cleared that up quickly, before the plane landed. I've been on teams that won five playoffs, and been MVP twice. But we lost in the World Series *four* times. The World Series isn't gravy. The Series is the ultimate prize, the reason we're here.

I think we felt to a man that the next season we would be ready to make that final step.

20

The amazing thing about the 1985 season is that it started off just that way—as if it was going to be The Fantasy Year. On paper, we were world champs when spring training began on March 1.

The front office had made what looked like the right moves. It was clear from the Series that our pitching staff needed help, so Ballard Smith and Jack McKeon, the Padres' vice president in charge of baseball operations, went out and got it. They traded with the White Sox for LaMarr Hoyt and signed Tim Stoddard as a free agent from the Cubs. Hoyt, a burly starter with excellent control, had won the Cy Young Award in 1983; Stoddard was the kind of reliever you like coming out of the bullpen—imposing, at six-seven and 250 pounds.

Our regular eight men were solid, but you can never have too much bench strength, so management signed two free agents—

Jerry Royster from Atlanta and Al Bumbry from Baltimore. Maybe, in retrospect, we could have been even more aggressive in that department. Fred Lynn was available. He could have helped us, and we would have maintained that continuity of acquiring quality free agents. But that's second guessing. To be honest, I thought when the season opened that we had enough to make a good run at repeating.

After four weeks of hovering between first and being a few games out, we settled into the top spot, and for the first half of the season held leads of from one and a half to four and a half games. All that time I never had the sense that we were secure. We were playing well—winning—but we could never put enough distance between ourselves and the pack. Like the Cubs against us during the playoffs, we were on top but couldn't deliver that knockout punch.

From the very beginning, there were signs of trouble. Most important, Alan Wiggins.

Alan missed the first week of the season with strained knee ligaments, and when he returned to the lineup, he couldn't seem to find the form that made him such an effective lead-off hitter for the team in 1984.

Wiggins was a crucial part of the Padres' success that season. He was the perfect lead-off man. While he batted only .258, he led the team in walks, stolen bases and runs scored. That combination translated into wins for us.

Three out of every four times Alan stole a base, he scored. He so intimidated the opposing pitchers that the man hitting second in our lineup—Tony Gwynn—saw mostly fastballs. Tony's .351 led the major leagues; with Alan on base, that average was .400.

In '85 Alan just wasn't the same ballplayer. He fell into a horrible slump after rejoining the team. Midway through the third week of the season, he was hitting only .054. Then came the road trip that began in Los Angeles. Alan never showed up for the first game. Nobody knew where he was. Eventually, through his agent, we learned that he had once again gotten involved with drugs, an old problem that we thought he had under control.

Outside of the short-lived strike, drugs were the number one off-the-field topic in baseball in 1985. There were the drug trials in Pittsburgh, with the parade of current and former major leaguers confessing their use of cocaine, and the continuation of Steve Howe's problems in Los Angeles, ending with his release. Before that, in 1982, there had been the trouble in Kansas City, leading to four Royals players being jailed. There had been flashes of trouble before; it was a crisis building.

While the use of illegal drugs has no place in any organization, it is especially incompatible with the image generated by the Padres. The team owner, Joan Kroc, has waged a public campaign against drug and alcohol abuse. She has never made a secret of her demand that her baseball team most represent the best of the community.

After Wiggins was arrested for cocaine possession in July 1982, he spent a month in a drug rehabilitation center and another month on suspension. Ballard Smith supported him in '82, but he made it clear that any recurrence of the problem would finish Alan with the Padres.

It looked as though Alan had his dependency whipped. He had the good seasons in 1983 and '84, and all that time he worked with the police and the community, traveling around and lecturing against the use of drugs.

Maybe some of that was a mistake; maybe there was just too much pressure on him. He was being held up as an example of the fallen being saved. That's a tough position. When he fell again, everybody felt let down.

I respect Alan Wiggins, both for what he has accomplished as an athlete and for the efforts he has made in his personal life. But I think he had a responsibility and he didn't live up to it. There were people here in the organization who were sympathetic to his situation. When he felt himself getting into trouble—falling back into that old hole—he should have come forward and asked for help. Instead he went back to drugs. Things could only get worse from there, and he ended up dropping out. In this business, where so many are relying on you on so many levels, you can't drop out.

The blame doesn't fall totally on his shoulders. He became a political issue, just as any player in trouble today would. Owners are on one side, afraid that drugs will get even more out of hand than they are now but terrified of hurting the image of baseball further by confronting the situation head on; the players association is on the other side, more concerned with protecting their own power base than with the good of their members. Both must become less obsessed with headlines and begin working together to save baseball.

It was interesting to watch as players around the league waited for the resolution of the Wiggins incident. He had suffered his relapse with drugs, was in a rehabilitation program, and everyone waited to see what would happen to him. After all, he had broken the rules by his own admission; how would he be punished? Players who might be in the same situation—or were approaching it—wanted to know.

The answer was that he wasn't punished. He missed a few weeks of the season and was traded to the Baltimore Orioles, where he went on to be a productive player. At least until the next emotional crunch. The only people punished were his club and teammates, who lost an integral part of their team, and the fans, who lost an exciting athlete and the chance to repeat as National League champions.

Most ballplayers wanted a firmer stand, even though the current agreement by players and owners forbids one. They talked of a fine of some meaningful amount—$50,000 or $100,000.

Money means a lot to an athlete. Take away ten percent of his salary and he'll think twice before shoving junk up his nose. Don't make it so easy for him to break the law.

Frankly, I would go further. The first time a player is found to be involved with drugs—proven to be taking or selling drugs—he would be suspended for a year. The second offense would get him barred for life from baseball.

This sounds tough, and that is exactly how I intend it to be. Baseball is not like other professions, like carpentry or acting or medicine. It occupies a very special place in society. Because of that place, the game is given all kinds of benefits—which began with the Supreme Court's decision in the 1920s that baseball was a sport and not a business, and therefore exempt from anti-monopoly legislation—and this continues today in the form of tax breaks and generous gifts from cities of prime land for stadiums.

It is more than just the legal and tangible favors. Baseball plays on its specialness to cultivate its position in the hearts and minds of the American people. We call ourselves the National Pastime and put ads on television dramatizing our importance as a tradition, even suggesting that going to games is the glue that keeps generations together. If we are going to tap those emotional veins to foster our own popularity, we in the game have an obligation to be clean—cleaner than the rest of society.

If we can't manage to achieve that ourselves, if the only way to get and keep ourselves clean is by establishing rules and enforcing them, that is what we must do. I am in favor of a voluntary testing program drawn up by the commissioner and the players association, one that has the members' support. We all have too much at stake not to act quickly and firmly.

Had such a plan been in effect a year ago, Alan Wiggins might still be playing second base for the San Diego Padres, and everyone concerned would be happier. Not that I am blaming Alan for all of the Padres' problems in 1985. Key injuries—especially to our pitching staff in August, when we were trying to make our late summer move—were at least as important. In 1984 the team was virtually injury free.

All this is part of a syndrome that has become familiar in sports over the past twenty years—the difficulty of duplicating a championship season.

While dynasties were once an active part of athletics, repeating even once as champion is almost unheard of today. It seems that there is an energy that can come over a relatively good team for a season and carry them to victory. Once on top, defending that position proves an awesome task. First, there is complacency in management—nobody wants to make too many changes in a winning combination—while the other teams in the same league are scurrying around, trying to improve themselves. With talent so evenly distributed, the balance of power can shift with the moving of a single athlete. A few key injuries can destroy a winning team's chemistry.

There is also an internal factor that isn't reflected in the team's roster. The desire to reach the top is simply greater than the desire to remain there. We all want passionately to prove we're the best—we bring that with us from the sandlots. Once we've done that, a certain hunger often abandons us, and that's all it takes to turn a winner into a loser.

For all these reasons, the paper championship of the Padres in 1985 never turned into the real thing. We struggled through the middle of the season, and just collapsed toward the end. Meanwhile, the Dodgers followed a sizzling Pedro Guerrero into first place; the season's dark horse, Cincinnati, forged into second; and we ended up fighting Houston for third.

Disheartening as losing is, it is part of the game. While I had never gotten comfortable with losing, in fifteen years of major league service, I have learned to live with it. Experience does that.

Instead of the playoffs and the World Series, I focused on smaller, more personal victories. I put some relatively satisfactory numbers on the board, completed a record string of 193 games between errors at first base, and played in my tenth All-Star Game.

Economically, the season was extremely successful. In addition to the usual run of well-paid speaking engagements, I entered into long-term arrangements with McGregor Apparel and Bankers Systems—by far the largest non-baseball contracts I ever signed.

The biggest is Bankers Systems. They are a company in St. Cloud, Minnesota, that got into the business of printing banking forms about thirty years ago, became the nation's largest in the field, and has expanded into financial planning, brokerage and investing services.

The man behind Bankers Systems is W. E. Clemens. Bill just about had the size to play sports for the tiny parochial school in North Dakota where he grew up, but he was much too small for college ball. He came away from his high school experience with an appreciation of how sports transcends barriers, and the unique position the athlete is in to reach people. Since 1980 he has used tennis players and golfers and now a baseball player to help sell his company's services.

This kind of association is becoming more and more common between athletes and business. Less visible than appearing on television drinking cola or eating cereal, it has the potential for more stable, prolonged income. Over the three years of my contract with Bankers Systems, I'll be making personal appearances and talking about their services to heads of the banking and business community.

Some people consider it strange that I spend so much time pursuing outside commercial interests after eight months of playing baseball—especially at this stage of my career, in the middle of a contract that earns me close to $1½ million a year. Why not, they ask, just kick back and relax for the winter?

First, I don't relax all that well. I can't remember the last time I sat down and watched an entire evening of television. I'm always concerned with wasting time. I want to take that time and do something with it, something educational, something profitable.

Partly that comes from being a professional baseball player since 1968. The time wasted in the course of a season—waiting in the hotel lobby for the bus to the park, waiting in airports for planes to take off, waiting at the batting cage for a chance to hit—is enormous. It is easy to get the feeling that your life is passing you by. Not just minutes or hours, but weeks and years.

It's not such a groundless fear. During his season, the player exists in a vacuum. For those eight months, everything is done on the club's schedule. Then it's finally the off season and he gives his body a few weeks to heal. Suddenly there are the holidays. By the time he throws out the Christmas tree, it's time to get ready for spring training. Blam! It's started all over again.

Before he knows it, he is at the end of his career and has given no thought to what comes next. He is prepared for nothing but baseball, and there no longer is any baseball. I've seen this happen over and over, and the results can be tragic. It is why I started PACE and PCCD, to slow down the process and help the athlete better prepare himself for "civilian" life.

For me, personally, it's been a concern almost since I entered baseball. From 1974 on, I began equating work away from the game with on-field success. It became easy to view each new account as if it were an award, a Gold Glove or an MVP trophy.

Now I'm building a marketing company the way I was building a baseball career a generation ago.

This is an especially important time for all of that. Though I am approaching the end of my baseball career and my skills are less than when I was in my prime, I am at my highest visibility. This is the time to capitalize on what I have accomplished on the field, not the time to sit back and smell the roses.

For those who ask me when enough is enough, I have no answer. It's not as if I need "X" amount of dollars to support a private jet and a yacht. While I like to think I live in style and comfort, luxury has never been my goal.

I would have to think there is something much more basic in my motivation, something not so different from the caution I felt as a high school student twenty years ago, when I was unwilling to focus all my energies on becoming a big-league ballplayer. College had to come first—an education that would guarantee me a livelihood in case I failed at sports.

This is the caution of the Catholic, working-class environment in which I grew up, an environment in which I learned very early to respect each and every dollar and what it buys.

When I think of those attitudes and how they were impressed upon me, I think of my mother. Though my father certainly embodied them, they came to me more directly from her. My dad worked long tours as a bus driver; his busiest times were my off times—my holidays and weekends. So it was often my mother with whom I spent my vacations. From her I learned that you could count on only what you could hold in your hand. Nobody bought the promise of pie in the sky in our house.

Millie Garvey:
"Everybody in my family worked. Execept my mother, of course. But she did her best to take care of the house.

"*Before her accident, she did work. As a little girl, she had her chores in the house and a job outside. She worked at the local cemetery, polishing the marble inside the mausoleums for 25¢.*

"*We lived comfortably. We had our own house, but everybody helped out. My brother worked. I worked in the advertising and public relations department of American Airlines. From our house on Long Island it was a two-hour trip into and out of Manhattan.*

"*My father worked especially hard. He operated a gas station. Long hours—six days a week. In 1948, when they moved from Long Island to Tampa, he ran a small motel.*

"*But as hard as he worked and as much money as he made, he gambled much of it away. It was a disease. Jai alai, racetracks of every kind. He wasn't a $1,000-a-day gambler, but it was in his blood. Whatever he had, he gambled.*

"*One night, while at the dog track, he had a heart attack and died. To the end, gambling!*

"*It was, I guess, part of what made me as conservative as I am. It rubbed off on Joe. We were both very cautious with our finances.*

"*We never preached to Steve about money, but I'm sure he was aware of our attitudes. He couldn't help but be affected. Security was very important in our house.*"

One of the most satisfying things that happened in the 1985 season had nothing to do with me directly. Late in the season, on a cool September night in Cincinnati, I was in the field when Pete Rose slammed a clean single to left-center, hit number 4,192 in his career, pushing him past Ty Cobb as baseball's all-time hit leader.

Once before I had been on hand when history was made. Early in the 1974 season, I was at first for the Dodgers in Atlanta when Henry Aaron hit the 715th home run of his career, passing Babe Ruth.

That night in Cincinnati will remain with me forever. Pete and I have always had one of those relationships that competing athletes sometimes share, one of respect and rivalry. There were all those seasons when the Dodgers and the Reds fought for the National League pennant, when Pete and I fought to get our 200 hits and help our team.

After Pete broke Cobb's record, he said something on television about this proving that you don't have to be smart or a super talent to make it in this world. In his own, very basic way, he put his finger on why he is so great. He is not a Willie Mays or a Roberto Clemente, a man of great natural talent. Rose has succeeded out of pure determination, and getting every ounce of ability from his body every time out.

Standing there, during that eternity of applause, as the city of Cincinnati poured out its love for its pug-faced warrior, watching him as he fought and fought for control of his emotions, finally letting them loose, the tears running down his face, I thought of a few lines of a speech once given by Teddy Roosevelt:

> The credit belongs to the man who is
> actually in the arena,
> Whose face is marred by dust and
> sweat and blood.
> A man who knows the great en-
> thusiasm and the great devotions
> Who in the end knows the triumph
> of high achievement
> And if he fails, at least fails while
> daring greatly.
> So that his place shall never be with
> those cold and timid souls
> Who know neither victory nor defeat.

When it's your moment, when you are the one receiving that outpouring, there is too much going on inside to permit you any degree of perspective. This was Pete's night; I was just an observer.

As I stood there, feeling the charge of all that emotion, it occurred to me that while sports are certainly about winning and losing, at a far more fundamental level it is about the relationship of an athlete and the people who come to cheer him on. It is about their ability to raise him to be better than he is, about his carrying the fantasies that they long ago traded in on more adult dreams, on two-car garages and kids in college and summer cottages by the lake.

All that cheering was a statement of satisfaction. Those people were really saying, "Pete, for the better part of a quarter-century you have carried our hopes and prayers out onto the field of competition. While you haven't always won, you've never given us less than 100 percent, and we love you for that."

Even more important, they were saying that those were qualities worth emulating. That even he was worth emulating.

That is a mighty weighty responsibility. It is what makes heroes out of athletes. I'm not so sure that a man who can hit .300 for 20 years or run 2,000 yards in a season deserves, mostly because of those abilities, to be a hero, but that is the reality. Sports belong to an area where performance is easily measured, and those who succeed are often given not only riches, but love and trust.

It is an opportunity for those so rewarded to make a special kind of contribution. It can be as simple as not betraying that trust. It can also go further—to live the kind of life that is worthy of emulation, to set an example worth following.

When I was a boy in Tampa, baseball players were my heroes, It was, to me at the time, the most wonderful idea in the world to grow up to be such a man as Gil Hodges, to be loved and respected, and emulated.

The idea affected me when I was in the minors; I wanted to behave the way I thought one of my Dodgers would behave, not only on the field but off. I carried that through when I came to Los Angeles. Visiting hospitals, getting involved with charity work—they all gave me pleasure, but also satisfaction, because I was fitting the profile.

If I, back then, had had the benefit of time and experience and maturity, I would have understood why some of my teammates were so unhappy with me. They had another picture of a ballplayer, or maybe they were just too occupied with holding on to their jobs to care. Regardless, they didn't share my perspective, and were furious at me because some fans thought less of them for that choice.

For what they suffered, I am sorry. Causing them grief was never my intention. I was only trying to follow what I thought was the right path.

That kind of decision isn't always easy. It's a lifetime occupation. Twenty-four hours a day, 365 days a year. I'd like to say 360 days, with five days off for good behavior, but you don't really get that.

One time in New York some of the guys wanted to go to Studio 54, and they thought it would be easier if I headed the group. It seemed harmless enough, so after the game we headed over. There happened to be a private party for Marvin Gaye at the club that night, but the man at the door recognized me and told us to go in.

We were at a table drinking beer when some guy came over and said that Marvin wanted to say hello. We went into a private room. It took me about five seconds to catch the scent of sweet, thick smoke. All I could see was the morning headline in the

Daily News: GARVEY ARRESTED IN DRUG BUST. I smiled and said hello all around, and got out as fast as I could.

No time off. Slip once and the whole thing blows up in your face. A lot of people don't want that kind of responsibility, and I understand that. But I like it. I think it's important.

Not that there aren't plenty of good role models around today. People like President Reagan, who has functioned so well under pressure, been shot, battled cancer, and come back every time. And Lee Iacocca, who managed to turn around a company on the brink of disaster. For us Catholics, the Pope.

But sports have a strong impact on young people, and not all of the examples athletes set are so positive. I figure there should be at least one straight arrow among the swingers.

That is, of course, what I'm talking about—offering people a choice.

In the twelve years that I have been a visible athlete I have traveled all through this country, and met people of all ages and economic situations. I've had the opportunity to talk with hundreds and hundreds of them, to listen to what's going on in their lives. Along with all the hand shaking and autograph signing, real communication happens in those encounters. Sometimes they consist of just a few minutes at an airport; other times they take place over years, as the same people keep turning up at their point in the schedule.

It has been gratifying to see how often those people and I share the same views—a basically conservative, methodical approach toward society and its flaws. It has been personally rewarding, and it has made me think there might be a future for me in public service.

The idea was first suggested about six years ago by Herbert Mizell of the *St. Petersburg Times*. It was appealing, and since then I have talked with members of both parties, and given the prospect serious consideration. More is needed. Can I, getting involved with politics this late, be effective? At what level would I enter, and when? Those questions must be answered.

One thing is certain: As a baseball player, I've learned that I love interacting with people, identifying problems and trying to solve them. (That's what PACE and PCCD are—my way of dealing with a specific problem of aging athletes.) I fully intend to continue those efforts. It may be on a small scale, as it is now. But if enough people like the choice that I offer—who I am and how I do things—maybe that scale will be larger. It's an idea I find very exciting.

When I think of who I am—how I got to be this way—I have to smile. A lot of it, of course, came from my parents. But a lot of it started at the age of seven with Roy Campanella and Pee Wee Reese, and especially Gil Hodges. I imbued them with all kinds of positive characteristics, with not only strength and speed but righteousness and kindness, the qualities that heroes in the 1950s seemed to have. I filtered everything I saw through the image of Gary Cooper playing Lou Gehrig in *The Pride of the Yankees,* all cast in the light of my own spiritual upbringing. I came away with a picture that, by the world's standards, was mostly fictional and somewhat naive, one that has led me into my share of difficulties and misunderstandings over the years.

Yet, as I approach the end of one career and contemplate the beginning of another, I find that the positive effects of my belief in that distortion of reality, that dream, far outweigh the negative.

Baseball, legend and religion—not such a bad combination to build on.

Appendix

STEVEN PATRICK GARVEY
(STEVE)

Born December 22, 1948, in Tampa, Florida.
Height, 5 feet, 9 inches.
Weight, 190 pounds.
Throws and bats righthanded.

Statistics and awards appear on the following pages.

YEAR	CLUB	AVG.	G	AB	R	H	2B	3B	HR	RBI	BB	SO	SB
1968	Ogden	.338	62	216	49	73	12	3	20	59	33	30	9
1969	Albuquerque	.373	83	316	51	118	18	2	14	85	15	48	9
	LOS ANGELES	.333	3	3	0	1	0	0	0	0	0	1	0
1970	Spokane	.319	95	376	71	120	26	5	15	87	34	51	13
	LOS ANGELES	.269	34	93	8	25	5	0	1	6	6	23	1
1971	LOS ANGELES	.227	81	225	27	51	12	1	7	26	21	33	1
1972	LOS ANGELES	.269	96	294	36	79	14	2	9	30	19	36	4
1973	LOS ANGELES	.304	114	349	37	106	17	3	8	50	11	42	0
1974	LOS ANGELES	.312	156	642	95	200	32	3	21	111	31	66	5
1975	LOS ANGELES	.319	160	659	85	210	38	6	18	95	33	66	11
1976	LOS ANGELES	.317	162	631	85	200	37	4	13	80	50	69	19
1977	LOS ANGELES	.297	162	646	91	192	25	3	33	115	38	90	9
1978	LOS ANGELES	.316	162	639	89	202	36	9	21	113	40	70	10
1979	LOS ANGELES	.315	162	648	92	204	32	1	28	110	37	59	3
1980	LOS ANGELES	.304	163	658	78	200	27	1	26	106	36	67	6
1981	LOS ANGELES	.283	110	431	63	122	23	1	10	64	25	49	3
1982	LOS ANGELES	.282	162	625	66	176	35	1	16	86	20	86	5
1983	SAN DIEGO	.294	100	388	76	114	22	0	14	59	29	39	4
1984	SAN DIEGO	.284	161	617	72	175	26	2	8	86	24	64	1
1985	SAN DIEGO	.281	162	654	80	184	34	6	17	81	35	67	0
	M.L. TOTALS	.298	2150	8202	1080	2441	415	43	250	1218	455	921	82

Game-Winning RBI: 1980—13, 1981—6, 1982—10, 1983—9, 1984—15, 1985—11. Total—64.

DIVISION SERIES RECORD

YEAR	CLUB. OPP.	AVG.	G	AB	R	H	2B	3B	HR	RBI	BB	SO	SB
1981	L.A. vs. Hou.	.368	5	19	4	7	0	1	2	4	0	2	0

LEAGUE CHAMPIONSHIP SERIES RECORD

YEAR	CLUB. OPP.	AVG.	G	AB	R	H	2B	3B	HR	RBI	BB	SO	SB
1974	L.A. vs. Pit.	.389	4	18	4	7	1	0	2	5	1	1	0
1977	L.A. vs. Phl.	.308	4	13	2	4	0	0	0	0	2	1	1
1978	L.A. vs. Phl.	.389	4	18	6	7	1	1	4	7	0	1	0
1981	L.A. vs. Mtl.	.286	5	21	2	6	0	0	1	2	0	4	0
1984	S.D. vs. Chi.	.400	5	20	1	8	1	0	1	7	1	2	0
L.C.S. Totals		.356	22	90	15	32	3	1	8	21	4	9	1

WORLD SERIES RECORD

YEAR	CLUB. OPP.	AVG.	G	AB	R	H	2B	3B	HR	RBI	BB	SO	SB
1974	L.A. vs. Oak.	.381	5	21	2	8	0	0	0	1	0	3	0
1977	L.A. vs. N.Y.	.375	6	24	5	9	1	1	1	3	1	4	0
1978	L.A. vs. N.Y.	.208	6	24	1	5	1	0	0	0	1	7	1
1981	L.A. vs. N.Y.	.417	6	24	3	10	1	0	0	0	2	5	0
1984	S.D. vs. Det.	.200	5	20	2	4	2	0	0	2	0	2	0
W.S.	Totals	.319	28	113	13	36	5	1	1	6	4	21	1

ALL STAR GAME RECORD

YEAR	CLUB. OPP.	AVG.	G	AB	R	H	2B	3B	HR	RBI	BB	SO	SB
1974	N.L. at Pit.	.500	1	4	1	2	1	0	0	1	0	1	0
1975	N.L. at Mil.	.667	1	3	1	2	0	0	1	1	0	0	0
1976	N.L. at Phl.	.333	1	3	1	1	0	1	0	1	0	0	0
1977	N.L. at N.Y.	.333	1	3	1	1	0	0	0	1	1	2	0
1978	N.L. at S.D.	.667	1	3	1	2	0	0	1	2	1	0	0
1979	N.L. at Sea.	.000	1	2	1	0	0	0	0	0	1	0	0
1980	N.L. at L.A.	.000	1	2	0	0	0	0	0	0	1	0	0
1981	N.L. at Cle.	.500	1	2	0	1	1	0	0	0	0	0	0
1984	N.L. at S.F.	.333	1	3	1	1	0	0	0	0	0	0	0
1985	N.L. at Minn.	.333	1	3	0	1	0	0	0	1	0	0	0
A.S.G.	Totals	.393	10	28	7	11	2	2	2	7	2	3	0

Signed by Los Angeles Dodgers organization following June free agent draft, 1968.

Signed as a free agent by San Diego Padres, December 21, 1982.

Most Valuable Player in National League, 1974.

Most Valuable Player in National League Championship Series, 1978, 1984.

Most Valuable Player in All-Star Game, 1974, 1978.